5/95

So Here I Am!
But Where Did I Come From?

So Here I Am!

But Where Did I Come From?

AN ADOPTEE'S SEARCH
FOR IDENTITY

by
Mary Ruth
Wotherspoon

PATE PUBLISHING
DETROIT, MICHIGAN

Additional copies of this book
may be ordered through bookstores
or by sending $19.95 plus $3.50
postage and handling to:
Publishers Distribution Service
6893 Sullivan Road
Grawn, MI 49637
(800) 507-2665

Publisher's Cataloging-in-Publication Data

Wotherspoon, Mary Ruth, 1924–
So here I am! but where did I come from?: an adoptee's search for
identity / Mary Ruth Wotherspoon—
Pate Publishing:
Detroit, Michigan.
p.   ill.   cm.
Includes bibliographical references and index.
ISBN: 0-9638488-0-1
1. Wotherspoon, Mary Ruth, 1924– 2. Adoptees–
United States–Identification. I. Title.
HV874.82.w68w68   1994
306.874'092[92][B]—dc20   93-85595

Printed in the United States of America.
Text Design by Heather Lee Shaw / PDS
10 9 8 7 6 5 4 3 2

With dearest love,
    To my children, grandchildren and
to all those yet to come.

Acknowledgements

Without the help and encouragement from my family and friends;

Without the help and patience of my husband;

Without the help and kindness from those who provided the necessary information needed for my successful search;

Without the help and nimble fingers of Kathleen MacRae (Secretarial Service);

. . . this book would never have been completed.

I thank them all with deepest appreciation.

Contents

PART THREE– THE PATE REUNION

PART FOUR– THE SASSER REUNION

PART FIVE– WASSI

PART SIX– SO HERE WE ARE!

CHAPTER

Preface

"You have such a happy tale to tell, why don't you write a book," I was asked over and over—and so I did!

Giving this suggestion much thought, I decided to write the story about finding my identity as a record for my family. While it is autobiographical, it is also written to help other adoptees who are wondering about their biological backgrounds. In telling about the many roads I took, encountering some long, some twisting, and some which were dead ends, I never completely gave up hope.

Not everyone's journey may turn out as happily as mine, but I hope my story will inspire and encourage those who feel a burning "need to know," or are curious enough about their heredity to travel courageously down the same road. Determination has its rewards!

So Here I Am!
But Where Did I Come From?

Part One

In the Beginning

Chapter One
Where Did I Come From?

"So, there you are!" declared the soft Southern drawl with unmistakeable glee. It was the first time I heard Lauretta's voice. A sudden shiver traveled from my toes to my ear resting against the phone. Immediately questions began racing through my mind. How does she know about me? Has she been wondering where I am while I've been searching for my unknown family? What does she look like? Do we look alike?

"I have found you at last," I cried joyously. "It's a miracle! When can we meet? We have so much to learn about each other." At that moment a wonderful relationship with my newfound family began.

I had another half-sister, Waudelle, but I had yet to phone her. My hand rested heavily on the receiver, and I felt the world lifting from my shoulders. I was trembling uncontrollably with excitement. After ten years, the search for my identity had been rewarded.

Suddenly, I was no longer an only child from Ohio, but one of three daughters born to a woman I had never known from North Carolina. I looked out at the fresh snow falling beyond the upstairs window of my studio/workroom in the colonial house my husband, Tom Swigart, and I built forty years before. At sixty years of age, I had discovered a new family—people who resembled me and knew from whence I came. My ancient, nagging questions could finally be answered.

Sinking into my chair, I let my thoughts drift back to the big grey stucco house with its blue shutters and entrance on the side; the house in which I grew up on Glenwood Avenue in Toledo. There I sat that day, staring—thinking—and remembering.

My mother's loving words echoed in my mind. "I chose you from among all of the babies I saw. You had big brown eyes

With my mother, Margaret Heyn Sanger. Age 3. 1927.

and such a winsome smile. I knew you were just the little girl I wanted! You were chosen. You were special. You were adopted." I felt warm and contented as she held me tightly in her arms and softly kissed me. Being told in this tender way at such a young age, I naturally accepted the fact that I was adopted. All that mattered was I belonged and was loved.

Then one day, Mother told me I had been born in Greenville, South Carolina, and my birth name was Julia Pate. I never thought much about this, as it seemed far removed from me, until she asked me several times, "You do think Mary Ruth is a prettier name than Julia, don't you?"

Always wanting to please, I dutifully answered, "Yes, Mother." I had some curiosity about my name, but I was too busy having fun to question. Sometimes I wondered secretly, "What's the difference?"—a favorite expression I often used, pronouncing it through my two separated, protruding front teeth, causing a slight whistle.

My adoptive parents were so excited to have a new baby that they picked my name from both sides of their families. I was named for my maternal grandmother, Marie Kaufman Heyn (Mary), and my two Aunt Ruths (Ruth); the one my mother's sister, the other my father's sister.

My childhood was filled with excitement and interest. I was a happy little girl, at play and in school, who wrote in her diary each night, "Had fun all day!" I considered myself lucky and very fortunate to have wonderful parents who gave me security, love and every advantage a child could have. Of course, I wondered about my identity from time to time, but I never dwelled upon it. Because the topic of adoption was not mentioned in those days, I never asked anyone about my heredity. I did not want to hurt my parents or any of my relatives, therefore the thoughts and questions I had were kept locked within me. "Does my birth mother ever think of me on my birthday, February 3rd? Where does she live, and what does she look like?" were a few of the secret questions that sometimes came to mind.

7

Chapter Two
About My Adoptive Parents

*M*y mother, Margaret Heyn Sanger, was of German descent and was born in Toledo (December 5, 1890), on 16th Street. "There's the house where I was born," she pointed out to me each time we drove downtown. "Some day that old, white frame house might be a famous landmark," she joked. Her mother was the only grandparent I ever knew. I was eight years old when Granny died. In addition to my mother's sister, Aunt Ruth Weil, there was a younger brother, Jamie, who lived to be only five years old. My grandfather, Albrecht Heyn, died before I was born.

Mother was a monologuist, poet and author of short stories. Because of the confusion between her name and Margaret Sanger, founder of the National Birth Control League (Planned Parenthood), she changed her name professionally to Margot Sanger. Mother performed on stage and radio, often using me as her live audience in order to practice her original monologues. These were impersonations of women from all walks of life in which she mimicked Southern, Jewish and French accents to perfection. Over and over she repeated her lines until I memorized many of them. Although Mother was just over five feet tall, her portrayal of the different personaiities she created was so vivid that her small stature was of no importance to her audience, just as props were hardly necessary to convey the setting of scenes.

I adored watching her "make up" before she went on stage. With a swift upward sweep of her hands, proceeding from the bottom of her throat, over her cheeks and across her forehead, she quickly applied her creams. Eyebrow pencil darkened her eyebrows, green eye shadow colored her eyelids, which accentuated her green eyes, and mascara blackened her lashes. A touch of rouge dotted her cheeks, red lipstick brightened her lips and—voilà! She was ready to perform. I loved peeking through the curtains from the wings. Some said she was better than Cornelia Otis Skinner. I was bursting with pride.

Often I was asked, "Have you inherited your mother's talent?" I only smiled and answered, "No, I like to draw and paint." I kept my adoption a secret.

With Mother, my life danced at a merry pace, and I never lacked for companions. Mother always welcomed my friends, but I never knew if they really came to see me or to be entertained by her. With family and friends we often gathered around the piano, as Mother "beat the box" with abandon, singing the musical hit tunes of the day. Once, when I was very small, she left me sitting in my tub, and I called out to her, "Please don't leave me, Mommie. You are so much fun!"

My father, Sigmond Sanger, was born in Szeben, Hungary (August 5, 1873) and came to the United States with his parents when he was a small boy. His family settled in Toledo where his three brothers, Walter,

William and Arthur, and his two sisters, Josephine and Ruth, were born. I recall his reminiscing with our Hungarian laundress, Suzie Dospoley, about digging for potatoes in the old country. He never forgot the hardships of the working class, and during the Depression never passed a poor man on the street without handing him

My father, Sigmond Sanger, c. 1927.

some pocket change. He was proud of being an old "newsboy," and worked hard to help put all of his brothers and sisters through college. In 1899, he received his law degree from the University of Michigan.

Uncle Walter became an engineer who then became superintendent of Public Works for the State of California. He oversaw the construction of Alcatraz Prison in San Francisco Bay. Uncle Will was a professor of mathematics at Worcester Polytechnic Institute, Massachusetts. Uncle Arthur, another engineer, was helping to build the causeway in the Florida Keys when a hurricane in the early 1920s swept him to his death. Aunt Jo, a pioneer school teacher, traveled west to teach in a one-room schoolhouse, later to return to

Toledo to live. Aunt Ruth, also a teacher, became head of the Home Economics Department of The Board of Education for The Toledo Public School System. My father's parents, Pauline Klein Sanger and Solomon Sanger, died before I was born.

Just as I adored watching Mother "make up" before a performance, Daddy's shaving ritual each morning was a source of utter fascination. I perched myself on the bathroom stool and waited with anticipation.

He began by mixing a foamy soapy lather in his shaving mug and then applying this to his face with a soft badger hair brush. Next, he opened a dark brown leather case. Inside were seven straight razors neatly arranged in a row with the day of the week engraved on each one; Monday through Sunday. I was allowed to choose the razor corresponding to that particular day. I felt very grown up. I watched him strop the blade on a taut leather strap, then scrape away the soapy suds from his cheeks and chin, leaving only his moustache untouched.

My father was twenty years my mother's senior when they married. It was Daddy's first marriage and Mother's second. Her first husband, Nathan Dreyfus, became ill and died one and a-half years after their marriage.

When Mother met Daddy, then a prominent attorney in Toledo, she joked, ". . . because he was so wrapped up in his law work, I had to learn Blackstone by heart in order to catch him."

Daddy was brilliant, dignified and sedate. His personality was oh, so different from Mother's light-hearted one. He exhibited a certain gruffness to those who did not know him well, but actually he was shy and had a soft spot in his heart, especially for me. How he tolerated some of my mother's shenanigans, I will never know.

One of her favorite pranks was to say to me, "Mary, let's pester Daddy," when he was sitting in his easy chair quietly reading his newspaper. Then we proceeded to kick the paper out of his hands. Oh, how we laughed, as he muttered under his breath, "Perfectly ridiculous!"

Mother was at her happiest when she retired upstairs on Sunday afternoons to "pound the typewriter," as she called it, creating her poems, stories and monologues. Daddy was "parked" downstairs in the sun room with his cigar-smoking, bridge-playing cronies. He loved cards, and I can remember him discussing bridge hands with friends, late into the night, long after I had been tucked into bed. My drowsiness, however, soon overtook the voices and laughter ascending the stairs.

Chapter Three
South of the Mason-Dixon Line

*W*hen I was a child, my parents and I spent many Christmases in Goldsboro, North Carolina, where my mother's sister and her family, the Lionel Weils, lived. Their white Southern mansion built on the crest of a hill was the most beautiful house I had ever seen. It had large columns reaching to the roof, with a wide veranda wrapping around three sides. The family gatherings with Aunt Ruth, Uncle Lee, my cousins Lee Jr., Helen Marie and Ruthie were festive occasions. We celebrated Hanukkah, the Jewish holiday, with prayers, candles and a special feast, which was not our usual Jewish custom in Toledo, where I was raised. In the large upstairs hall of the Weil house, there was always a decorated Christmas tree with presents underneath. Therefore, our holiday celebrations in the South were twofold. (I wonder now, in retrospect, if the Christmas tree had been arranged for my sake.) I missed the snow we left behind in Ohio, and I could not imagine how Santa managed to arrive in his sleigh without it.

My cousin, Ruthie, was seven months

younger than I, and we became inseparable. Under the watchful eye of her governess, Georgia McTier, we played in the park at the end of the street and searched for four-leaf clovers in the wooded lowlands next to the house. Georgia always managed to find the first one.

Uncle Lee took Ruthie and me to the large Weil Brothers Department Store. There were racks of print dresses, jackets and coats and tables of assorted shoes. Wooden cases with glass counter tops, filled with purses, gloves and sparkling jewelery, lined the aisles on the main floor. As purchases were made, we watched with fascination the small oval "money changers" shoot through the elevated pneumatic glass tubes to the upstairs business office and woosh back to the ground floor, returning with the correct amount of change to the waiting customer. To us, this was pure magic.

One day we visited Uncle Lee's tobacco farms, which were unforgettable to a small Yankee girl. Certain aromas have the power to evoke the past, and now every time I smell tobacco I remember the pungent odor of huge golden-brown tobacco leaves hanging up to dry in old wooden barns. We watched as the farmers sorted and bundled the leaves, and we listened as Uncle Lee explained the process of drying and shipping tobacco to the manufacturers to be made into cigarettes.

My days spent south of the Mason-Dixon line were happy ones, yet I felt slightly different from my cousins. I could see that I did not resemble them, and I wondered if my Northern accent was the only other difference. I can still hear Ruthie calling for Georgia's help when Ruthie's big brother Lee Jr. ("Sloppy" was his nickname, for reasons that were obvious) was chasing her through the house.

"Turn me loose! Georgia, make Sloppy turn me loose," she cried in her shrill Southern drawl. These were among the early memories which made the South so rich for me.

Chapter Four
I Want to Look Like Me!

I grew to be taller than my parents, resembling neither one. When anyone asked, "Where did she get those big brown eyes?," Mother would wink at me and say, "From her father, of course," whose eyes also happened to be brown.

My next door neighbor, Jayne, who was two years older than I and therefore presumed to be wiser, somehow knew about my adoption. She suggested with conviction that I was a dark-eyed Spanish Princess. These fantasies of my childhood lingered with me for many years.

One of my favorite poems was:

"<u>Everybody Says</u>
Everybody says, I look just like my mother.
Everybody says, I'm the image of Aunt Bea.
Everybody says, my nose is like my father's,
But I want to look like me."

When I was four years old, Mother and I sailed across the Atlantic on the Ile de France to spend the summer in Caboure, France. Mother performed on shipboard and in Caboure. I rode the donkey on the beach and, with my French playmates, watched the Punch and Judy shows in the park. Upon our return, Daddy surprised us by meeting our ship in the New York Harbor. He stood on the deck of the tugboat that came to help dock the Ile de France and precariously climbed aboard, clinging to a rope ladder that had been lowered to him. Because he was not athletically inclined, it was an extraordinary feat and touched our hearts with his effort to be the first to greet us.

When I was a young teenager, Mother, Daddy and I took a cruise to Bermuda during my spring vacation. What a lucky little girl I was. Did I realize at such a young age how fortunate I was to be able to travel extensively? Probably not, but as I grew older I appreciated more and more the many privileges provided me by my family.

Chapter Five
Heredity versus Environment

*M*y early education consisted of public and private schools. The first two years were divided between Glenwood and Smead Schools in Toledo. During the third grade I was whisked off to New York City to live with Mother while she performed on stage and radio. I attended Calhoun School, learned about the Iroquois Indians, and roller-skated in Riverside Park. I missed Daddy, my own backyard and my friends. Returning to Toledo, I continued my schooling at Maumee Valley Country Day and Glenwood Schools.

My special friend, Maxine Behr, and I had a lot in common. We were both "only" children, and our birthdays were two days apart. Her nickname was "Mickey," therefore mine also became "Mickey." We loved to draw, and spent Saturday afternoons drawing and painting at each other's houses. When we grew older, we attended art classes together at the Toledo Museum of Art. Fond memories reflect the times we spent giggling, exchanging secrets and dressing alike.

As I began to mature, it became apparent that my mother's constant attentions had a profound influence on me, causing my continual dependence upon her. Therefore, after one year at Scott High School in Toledo, I was sent to Kingswood School Cranbrook, a boarding school for girls in Bloomfield Hills, Michigan, from where I graduated in 1942. Being away from home helped to develop my independence and broaden my education. My artistic talent was recognized, and I was given special privileges to attend life-drawing classes at the nationally acclaimed Cranbrook Institute of Art across the lake. In my senior year at Kingswood, I became art editor of the yearbook.

Because of my love for children, and wanting to establish myself in a profession, I decided to become a teacher. The following fall I entered Wheelock College in Boston which specialized in Elementary Education. One of my most enlightening classes was a child development course in which was debated the relative importance of heredity versus environment. Which one played the most significant part in the development of a child?

This controversial topic, once again, stirred my thoughts about my own identity. Who was I, this girl from the South being brought up in the North? Had I not been blessed to have had parents who lavished me with love, and unselfishly provided me with a wonderful education; who had given me piano, swimming, horseback riding, dancing and art lessons; had my teeth straightened and bought me beautiful clothes, would I have been living on a tobacco farm in the Carolinas, or would I have been that imaginary Spanish Princess?

In my formative years, my parents molded me to conform to the environment in which we lived. But, I realized my heredity also played an important part in my development. Who is my birth mother? Am I like her? Do I have siblings, and do I look like them? I constantly peered into people's faces, and found myself obsessed about family resemblances. Maybe that is why, in later years, I became interested in painting portraits.

While I was at Wheelock, Mother made arrangements for her radio broadcasts and live stage performances to take place in Boston in order to be near me. She was billed as <u>Margot Sanger and her Theater of Imagination</u>. At the Copley Plaza Hotel, she was on the same playbill with Victor Borge, and they were equally superb.

Boston swarmed with servicemen during World War II and, in spite of the war, it was an exciting time for college students. The rise of Hitler and the Jewish Holocaust caused my mother's constant reminder, "Mary, remember, you do <u>not</u> have a drop of Jewish blood in you." She was fearful that Hitler would invade the United States. Her concern for me, even though the danger was remote, was thought-provoking, because I loved my parents, relatives and our many Jewish friends. This made me realize the terrible forces of meaningless discrimination being forced upon the world by Hitler. It also made me realize how different I was and increased my curiosity about my natural background.

Chapter Six
Becoming Tom's Bride

I left college to become Mrs. Eugene Thomas Swigart, Jr. Tom had been a part of my life since high school. I first noticed him playing basketball in a neighbor's backyard when we were freshmen. His agile athletic build, bright blue eyes and engaging smile caught my attention. He carried my books home from school and, before long, became a part of our family. Mother and Daddy adored him. Because Daddy never learned to drive, Tom was often his chauffeur. He also ran errands for Mother, taught me how to drive, and captured our wire-haired fox terrier, Hankie, whenever he escaped from his pen. Tom was always there for us. He was the brother I never had. He was forever telling me he loved me, but I was too busy with my other teenage crushes to pay much attention. I recalled a time when I caught his bright blue eyes, along with two big brown ones, peering at me over the railing of the next door neighbor's porch as I was kissing a date good night at my front door. Tom and his

black Labor-
ador retriever,
Pete, thought
they had been
hidden from
view. He al-
ways wanted to
be first in my
life. Later I
learned he had
told his parents,
"I have met the
girl I'm going to
marry."

When he en-
listed in the ser-
vice, I realized
I would not be
hearing his
cheerful whistle
coming up the

*Cadet Eugene Thomas Swigart, Jr.,
U. S Army Air Corps, 1944.*

front walk each day, nor would I be seeing that stray
lock of blond hair drooping over his forehead nor the
familiar white silk scarf carelessly wrapped around his
neck. My "brother" had grown up, and it dawned on
me how much I would miss him. It was then I knew I
had fallen hopelessly in love.

Tom became a cadet in the U.S. Army Air Corps and
was stationed at Courtland Field, Decatur, Alabama,
where he served as a nose gunner on a B-24. He looked
handsome in his uniform with his silver wings pinned
to his jacket. His bright blue eyes twinkled when he
smiled.

On Christmas Day 1943, my parents announced our
engagement. We planned to be married in Alabama as
soon as Tom received his promised three-night pass.

In my white satin wedding gown, February 25, 1944.

In late February, our families made the long train trip to Decatur where we stayed in an old hotel. Our rooms were dingy and cramped. My white satin wedding gown and veil, which Mother had the foresight to have made for me when our engagement was announced, hung limply from an exposed ceiling pipe. Our impatient waiting finally came to an end on Friday, February 25, 1944.

Tom attended the First Congregational Church in Toledo, and I, at a young age, the Temple. As I grew older, my parents exposed me to a presbyterian church and, while at Kingswood School Cranbrook, I attended an episcopalian church. Where we were married was not as important as having a spiritual rather than civil ceremony. Therefore, we were grateful to have found a warm-hearted Methodist minister whose kindness enabled us to be wed in his church on such short notice.

Our wedding ceremony was performed in the chapel, with Tom's sister, Sally, my maid of honor; Ben Weeks, an Army Air Corps friend of Tom's, his best man; our parents; a handful of servicemen, and the taxi cab driver attending the wedding. Mother and Daddy hosted a festive dinner in the old hotel dining room. After many toasts and happy tears, we hurriedly escaped to the waiting taxi cab, where we were taken to another more up-to-date hotel for the first of our three blissful nights. It

Tom, ready to fly Courtland Field, Decatur, Alabama, 1944.

was mandatory that Tom report to the field each morning by six o'clock, ready for flight training. This was our honeymoon—not exactly what we had in mind, but after all, it was wartime.

Chapter Seven
The Way of the War

I was a young war bride who tagged along with her husband when he was transferred from Courtland Field, Decatur, Alabama, to Lowery Field, Denver, Colorado, and then to Westover Field in Holyoke, Massachusetts. Like other war brides, I lived in boarding houses, shared bathrooms, cooked on hot plates and waited for my husband to return.

In Decatur, our living quarters offered little privacy and many surprises. One evening when Tom was taking a bath, he suddenly saw our landlady, Mrs. Chenault, open the door and back into the bathroom chattering loudly. She was showing her accommodations to another young Army Air Corps couple. Tom's eyes met theirs in mutual embarrassment as Mrs. Chenault calmly walked out, unaware that her tenant was in the tub. It was the way of the war: some good times, some bad, but forever memorable.

When I became pregnant, my doctor recommended I return to Toledo toward the end of my confinement to live with my parents until the baby was born. By this time Tom was stationed at Westover Field. My father made the train trip to Holyoke to escort me home. It was unlike him to show such outward concern, and it touched me deeply.

Our first child, Thomas John, was born April 12, 1945—the day Franklin Delano Roosevelt died. Tom received a three-day pass to visit his little son and me, and six weeks later another pass to drive us back to Holyoke. We were blissfully happy with our new baby. Our only problem was the diaper dilemma. With neither disposable diapers, automatic washing machine, nor dryer, I waited for Tom's help to wring out the dozens of diapers by hand and hang them up to dry. It was a laborious daily task.

On May 7, 1945, the war ended in Europe. Tom was told he would be transferred to Walla Walla, Washington. In the event that he might be sent to the Far East, and because of poor housing conditions in Walla Walla, we decided this was not the place for a young mother and baby. Therefore, little Tommy and I would return to Toledo. This time my mother and my mother-in-law offered to help me make the long drive back with their new grandson. I planned to live with my family while awaiting Tom's return and the end of the war with Japan.

The two grandmothers arrived in Holyoke on the weekend Tom was to receive his orders for his departure. We had made arrangements for our mothers to share a room in the boarding house in which we lived. There was only one problem—the room had a double bed. Being good sports and being fond of each other, they joked, "Well, it's only for the weekend. We'll manage."

However, that was not the case. It turned out our mothers were cloistered in one room, sharing one bed and wearing the same clothes for two weeks. I was elated Tom's orders were delayed, but our mothers were a bit on edge. How they managed to keep their sense of humor was hard to comprehend. We saluted them for performing their war duties by volunteering help and demonstrating patience to their appreciative family.

Chapter Eight
Our Family Grew

*W*orld War II ended August 14, 1945. The country rejoiced to see the end of Hilter's reign in Germany and Japan's surrender. Tom returned home safely to Toledo without serving overseas.

With our young son we moved into a little white bungalow, and Tom completed his degree in Business Administration at the University of Toledo. Our family increased with another son, Stephen Herrick (Steve) and then a daughter, Margaret Elizabeth (Meg). All three of our children were blond, blue-eyed and resembled their father. Everyone remarked how dominant the Swigart strain was. But secretly I wondered, what about my side of the family? What do they look like? Only our border collie, Toby, and I had brown eyes. I had given up hope of ever having a baby who looked like me. It was a total surprise when our last child, another daughter, was born with dark hair and brown eyes. We named her Mary Catherine (Mimi), and we were elated.

In 1956, Tom began his own business

with a friend, Charles Donald Werner, Jr. Tom was the president in charge of sales, and Don, vice-president, was the chemist. They manufactured and distributed industrial detergents for commercial use, and called it Spartan Chemical Company.

As the company expanded and our family grew, we needed a larger home, so we decided to build a colonial house in the Village of Ottawa Hills, a suburb of Toledo. We also bought 320 acres of wooded land on one of the six Spectacle Lakes near Lewiston, Michigan, with two other couples, the Baileys and Zerners. We named it Swig-

Our house in the Village of Ottawa Hills, Toledo, Ohio, 1953.

Swig-Bai-Ze on Spectacle Lake, Lewiston, Michigan, 1951.

Bai-Ze. It was accessible to fishing, hunting and skiing. When our children were young, we spent family vacations in rustic log cabins there. Besides Tom's love for the outdoors, he played polo and became a private pilot. He often flew from Toledo to Swig-Bai-Ze for weekends. Our lives were happy and busy with dogs, cats, other assorted pets, and the many activities revolving around our children.

When Steve was a baby, Martha Grant came to work for us. Without wonderful Martha, we could not have managed. She helped us in every way—cleaning, washing and caring for our family for nearly forty years. She was faithful and true, and we all loved her. After our children were

Martha Grant with Steve, 1949.

Easter, 1954.

grown, I painted her portrait which now hangs in her home.

While Tom poured most of his energy into his thriving business, I became involved in Junior League activities, community volunteering, serving on boards and taking art courses at the Toledo Museum of Art.

Christmas, 1953.

I was asked to illustrate a children's book written by Janet Haskin, which was published in 1957. It was titled <u>Johnny Bushytail</u>, the adventures of a gadabout squirrel. Since our children were still young, I delighted in reading them the story, and they, in turn, offered suggestions for illustrations.

"Oh, Mommie, draw a picture of Johnny Bushytail when he was sick after having eaten too many nuts, and

34

Tom playing polo (left), c. 1959 - 1960.

his Mommie had to give him medicine and put him to bed," or, "Mommie, draw Johnny Bushytail wearing his little red cap, muffler and red jacket." What vivid imaginations children have for illustrations in just the right places.

Tom and I told our children about my adoption. While surprised, they accepted this information without question. I was their mother who loved them, and that was all that mattered. How I envied the memories they would have of growing up with each other, and of sharing the same heredity and environment.

This left me misty-eyed, and I often thought about what I might have missed by not having brothers and sisters. But there was no need for our children to wonder, and I was thankful about that. Our family flourished.

Pheasant shoot with the Urschels and the Lumms,
c. 1960.

Chapter Nine
My First Amended Birth Certificate

*A*s our children matured, I keenly observed their mental and physical development. Thoughts about my own identity never left me, and the curiosity about my heredity grew stronger.

My father died two Christmases before our second son, Steve, was born, January 26, 1948. Uncle Lee Weil died a few weeks after Steve's birth, and Aunt Ruth Weil several years before. In the late spring of 1948, my mother gave me an amended birth certificate issued on May 27, 1948. I was twenty-four years old. Although she never said it, I believe she felt it was necessary by then for me to have an official identity, as she was rapidly losing those closest to her.

It was a standard certificate of birth issued from the State of South Carolina. It stated:

Name: Mary Ruth Sanger
Born: February 3, 1924
Time: 9:40 p.m. Weight: 6-3/4 lbs.
Sex: Female
Birthplace: Greenville, South Carolina

37

Father's Name: Sigmond Sanger
Race: White
Born: Szeben, Hungary
Occupation: Attorney-at-Law
Age on Last Birthday: 73*
Mother's Name: Margaret Heyn Sanger
Race: White
Born: Toledo, Ohio
Occupation: Housewife
Age on Last Birthday: 57*
Current Address: 2624 Glenwood Avenue, Toledo, Ohio
Doctor in Attendance: L. W. Boggs
(Signed) Thomas P. Lesesne, Assistant State Registrar.

*These were the ages of my adoptive parents when my mother applied for this amended birth certificate in 1948. (My father had died in 1946 at the age of 73.)

There was no mention of my birth name, Julia Pate, but the doctor's name caught my attention. Is he still alive and did he have my birth records? I wondered. I was happy to have the amended certificate, but also determined to try to find the original in order to learn my birth mother's name. I felt someday I would pursue this unsolved puzzle, but now was not the time.

Chapter Ten
Family Travels

*T*om and I traveled a great deal, both with and without our children. His business took him throughout the U.S., Mexico, South America, Australia and Europe, and I accompanied him whenever possible. Mother predicted, "Tom, someday you will clean up the world."

Anne and Peter Overstreet, Mexico, 1981.

He certainly made an effort to do so, and I was proud of what he had accomplished. He was on the Board of Directors of the International Sanitary Supply Association (ISSA) for several years. In the mid-'70s, he was elected President of the Association. Now, our sons, Tom and Steve, are carrying on with the still-growing Spartan Chemical Company business.

With President-elect Ronald Reagan at the
International Sanitary Supply Convention,
Chicago, Illinois, 1975.

Mother, Steve, Mimi, Meg, Tommy, Mary Ruth
and Tom departing for a Mediterranean Cruise,
1961.

We took many family vacations—skiing trips to Northern Michigan and Colorado, and to the warmer climates of Florida and the Bahama Islands. In the summer of 1961, Mother treated all of us to a Mediterranean cruise. We sailed on the S.S. Constitution from New York to Nice, occupying three staterooms; Tom and I in one, our sons in another, and our daughters sharing one with their grandmother.

After three days at sea, Meg came running up on deck to announce in a terrified voice, "I left my retainer for my teeth in the bathroom and now it is missing. I think Grandma threw it in the trash or maybe flushed it down the toilet."

Our first thought was, all of the orthodontist's work down the drain. Bless the crew! They searched the bowels of the ship until miraculously it was found.

After stopping at Gibraltar and Majorca, our ship sailed into the Bay of Naples for a day, setting sail again at midnight. When our teenage sons learned the Beatles were performing that very evening in Naples, nothing could have kept them from attending the performance.

"No problem, Dad. We'll be back in plenty of time before our departure," they exclaimed confidently.

No one took into account the amount of traffic they would encounter. Blasts from the ship's whistles sounded warnings for our departure, but the boys were nowhere in sight.

Tom grabbed his passport and shouted, "I'm going to look for them, and we'll meet you in Rome, the next port of call!"

We were terrified. What could have happened? An accident? It was frightening to suspect the worst.

As Tom raced down one gangplank, he happened to glance toward another gangplank and saw the boys rushing up it. We were thankful for the close call, and so relieved to see them that they were not reprimanded.

After Rome, Pompeii and Genoa, we disembarked at Nice, where Mother had rented a villa overlooking the Mediterranean. From our terrace we looked to the east toward Monte Carlo and to the west toward Cannes. The sea was directly below. Early each morning we heard the tiny fishing boats chug-chugging out to sea, returning at sunset with their catch.

We toured southern France and Italy. Our children made friends with French children and learned to converse with them to some degree. Mother, being fluent in French, and I, having been exposed to it most of my life, found it a treat to be able to communicate. Madame Nelly Van der Velde, our housekeeper, was there to aid us at all times, and became a good friend. I can still hear Mother calling, "Madame Nelly, oú êtes-vous?" And she would come running.

Via England, we sailed home on the Queen Elizabeth from Southampton to New York. Tommy stayed to tour Ireland with his friend, Mike Davies, and his father, Bob, whom we had met in London. Our other three children sailed home with Mother, Tom and me.

It was the Queen Elizabeth's last voyage across the Atlantic. She creaked and groaned, as if she knew her age and sensed her time was up. On the other hand, our children, being young, hale and hearty, took the liberty of ordering steaks, French fries and hot fudge sundaes in their cabin all times of the day or night. Feeling very grown up without their older brother on board, they imagined themselves seasoned travelers. We hoped all four of our children had absorbed some education and worldliness from our fabulous trip.

Chapter Eleven
Death Comes to My Adoptive Mother

In March 1967, my mother died at the age of seventy-six. Her life ended quickly from a heart attack.

"I never want to be a burden to you," she often told me. How could she have been?

Oh, Mother! I grieved my loss.

Just before her death, I told her I had decided to complete my college education.

"I want to set a goal for myself and earn my degree in Fine Arts and French." She was delighted to hear this.

In the fall, at age 43, I became a college student

My graduation from the University of Toledo, December, 1976. I was already a grandmother.

again. My credits were transferred from Wheelock College and from the Toledo Museum of Art, where I had taken studio courses for many years. Nearly ten years later, in December 1976, I received a Bachelor of Arts Degree in Fine Arts and French from the University of Toledo. By this time, I had become a grandmother, and I felt a sense of accomplishment in both departments. The following spring, Mimi received her law degree from the University of Toledo.

Two years later in December 1979, as a tribute to my mother's memory, I published a book of her writings titled, <u>Poems and Prose</u>. I selected and edited her poems, short stories and monologues and illustrated the section that included her stories for children. During her lifetime, many of her writings appeared in magazines and newspapers. In 1950 she published a small book of her favorite monologues titled, <u>Anne to Zonia</u>.

Her "joie de vivre" will remain my most vivid and cherished memory of this unique woman . . . my mother!

Chapter Twelve
"Can He Be Ours?"

I took several trips to Europe with a friend, Anne Overstreet, and a cruise to the Greek Islands with Anne and our friend, Dr. James Southworth, who was an English Professor and Head of the English Department at the University of Toledo. Our husbands were too busy to travel for pleasure, but unselfishly encouraged us to pursue our interests in art and ancient culture.

Jimmy, being nearly 80 years old and very knowledgeable, was a delightful companion. We could hardly keep up with him, as he rode the donkey up and down the steep slopes of Santorini, then called back to us upon reaching the ship, "I'll meet you in the lounge at six o'clock for cocktails." By the time we rinsed off the day's dust and made ourselves presentable, Jimmy had finished his martini and was ready to dance with each of us.

Years later, I spent many "grandmother" ski vacations in Colorado with my friends, Peggy Bailey and Jeane Barnum. Sometimes the grandfathers, Tom, Paul and Tony joined us. I find skiing to be a most exhilarating sport, and I continue to ski to this day.

When Tom and I became grandparents, most of our grandbabies were born with blond hair and blue eyes, all resembling the Swigart family. Then one day, our grandson, Todd, was born with big brown eyes and high cheekbones.

"Can he be ours?" I exclaimed. "He must be a throw-back to my ancestry." I seriously wondered. Can that be? It was then that my curiosity about my heredity reached its peak.

Several years later, my Aunt Ruth Sanger died. There was no one left in the family now to be hurt by my determination to find my roots, so I felt free to begin my search.

In the beginning I was reluctant to discuss my plans with anyone outside of my immediate family, as I was not accustomed to talking about being adopted. It was not a subject often mentioned when I was growing up. I felt secure in that I was the daughter of the Sangers, was loved and that was all that mattered. There were

Cruising the Greek Islands with Dr. James
Southworth and Anne Overstreet, July, 1977.

times, however, when school and medical forms had to be filled out and questions about my biological background had to be answered.

"Is there a history of cancer, heart disease, diabetes or alcoholism in your family?" I was asked again and again. Of course, I did not know. I was too embarrassed to admit I was adopted, and too afraid of hurting my parents by questioning them, so I made up the answers to these questions. I lived with my secret most of my life. It was not until our children and grandchildren were born that I was ready to seek the unknown.

"Grandmother" ski vacations with Peggy Bailey and Jeane Barnum, Colorado, c. 1980's.

Part Two

Searching

Chapter Thirteen
Beginning to Search

*W*ith Tom's help and our children's encouragement I began my search in January, 1974. My initial effort was to obtain a copy of my original birth certificate which would bear my birth mother's name.

Because of my reluctance to discuss my plans openly, Tom and I hired Pinkerton investigators. All we had to aid them was my birth name, date and place of birth. I knew some adoptees did not even have this much information about themselves, so I felt lucky. The investigators checked medical records at hospitals and records at the Bureau of Vital Statistics in Greenville and Columbia, South Carolina. They were told these records were either destroyed or sealed and were impossible to obtain. One investigator interviewed the Lucas County Probate Court Judge in Toledo, and established the fact that my adoption papers were recorded in Toledo, but were confidential. However, since Judge Ludeman, had known my late father, Sigmond Sanger, he agreed to review the file, but at a later date. We waited!

The Pinkerton investigators then suggested a possible connection between Greenville, South Carolina, where I was born and Goldsboro, North Carolina, where my relatives, the Weils, had lived. This seemed doubtful to me at first, but the question arose: Why did my mother travel all the way to Greenville, South Carolina, in 1924 in order to adopt a baby, when many babies must have been available closer to Toledo? Is there a connection? Was this a private adoption?

The continued rechecking of records in Greenville, South Carolina, by the Pinkerton investigators with no successful leads, left me completely frustrated. Then, in July 1980, an investigator again interviewed Judge Ludeman at the Lucas County Probate Court in Toledo. This time the judge agreed to see me. I could not believe my good fortune. My daughter, Mimi, having become a successful attorney in Toledo, knew Judge Ludeman. This must have played an important part in his decision. With much anticipation, and yet a certain amount of apprehension, Mimi and I visited with him in his chambers. He could not have been kinder when he presented us with copies of my adoption papers.

Poring over the many pages, I found my birth name, Julia Pate, recorded, but there was no mention of my birth mother's name. My adoption took place in Toledo on March 12, 1927, three years after I was born. Another puzzling question arose: Why did my adoptive parents wait until I was three years old before legally adopting me? I knew they loved me, and I knew I had lived with them during the first three years of my life because I had proof of this. My mother kept a baby book detailing my daily development from six weeks old through my early years in school. There were photographs, samples of hair, baby teeth, medical records, weights and heights, first drawings, first writings, first sayings, and so forth. This was her precious book, which she allowed me to leaf through when I was sick in bed. It was a special treat to keep me quiet and amused, and I loved it. Now, it is my treasured memory.

Why then, this three year gap in my young life? My adoption records stated I was held a ward at the Lucas County Children's Home under the guardianship of Walter F. Brown. Mr. Brown was my father's law partner and former Postmaster General of the U.S. under President Herbert Hoover.

This was a shocking discovery for me. What did it mean to be held a ward? And why? I hoped to find out.

Chapter Fourteen

Agencies, Organizations and Search Groups

$\mathcal{T}$oward the end of 1980 and the beginning of 1981, the Pinkerton investigators continued searching in the Wake County Court House in Raleigh, North Carolina, the Children's Home Society of North Carolina in Greensboro, North Carolina, and the Court House records of Wayne County, Goldsboro, North Carolina. No records for Julia Pate were located.

I was informed about library and news articles stating names of search groups and agencies formed to help adoptees and birth parents with their searches. I devoured these articles and acquired as much information as possible. Most stated that adoptees have identity information rights to:

1. Obtain original birth certificate (not amended),
2. knowledge of origin (heredity back ground),
   a. name given at birth
   b. ethnic and religious background
   c. medical and social background

3. legal access to adoption and birth records,
4. and personal contact with birth parents and families.

With the knowledge of these rights, I was encouraged to continue my search.

In 1982, I began corresponding with many of these search groups and agencies throughout the U.S. by letter and through telephone calls. My postage stamps dwindled and my phone bills increased. Those contacted were: Adoptees and Birthparents in Search (South Carolina), Adoptees Liberty Movement Association (ALMA), Adoptees Searching, Adoptees Search Rights Association, Adoptees Together, Children's Bureau of South Carolina, International Soundex Reunion Registry (ISRR), Operation Identity, Orphan Voyage, Yesterday's Children. Many wanted membership fees in exchange for their services, many did not. Some were helpful, some were not. They all agreed adoptees had the right to know their identity, but there were laws.

Only five states in 1979 allowed this "right to know." They were Alabama, Kansas, Minnesota, New Jersey and South Dakota, none of which applied to me. Other states required a court order to obtain an original birth certificate. Today, at least twenty-two states have a reunion registry—a file of birthparents and adoptees over the age of eighteen or twenty-one who are seeking each other. Reunions are possible when both sides have signed up, allowing the state to hand over names and addresses. Several states have "search and consent" rules, which permit adult adoptees to contact state social service departments and request a search for birthparents. Some use an intermediary system. In Washington State, for example, a birth mother or adoptee can have a court-appointed person perform the search. A reunion is arranged only by mutual consent.

Support groups exist across the country. Many branches require attendance at several meetings before they will share search advice.

The general trend when I was adopted was for adoption records, adoption agency records, investigation reports and original birth certificates to be permanently sealed once an adoption was finalized. I was told, again and again, the purpose of sealed records was to protect the privacy of the adoptive and birth families, as well as shield the child from the stigma of illegitimacy. Even though these were laws, I felt this did not affect me now that I was a grown woman and my adoptive parents were no longer living. But, of course, I did not know if this would affect my biological family should I find them.

When many well-meaning friends learned how serious I was about my search, they questioned, "Aren't you afraid of what you'll find . . . Do you really want to know . . . Aren't you contented with your life . . . You had such a privileged upbringing with devoted parents." This was true, I was a fortunate child. I will be grateful forever to my parents, but that isn't the point. I wanted and needed to know who I was and from where I came.

Chapter Fifteen
Do Family Servants Know Secrets?

*S*o many questions filled my mind:

- What are my birth parents' names?
- Were both of them living at the time of my adoption?
- What was their reason for giving me up?
- Were my birth parents married to each other?
- Was either married to someone else?
- From what state and city do my birth parents come?
- What are the ages of my birth parents?
- Do I have siblings?
- What are their occupations?
- What are their educational backgrounds?
- What are their medical histories?
- What are their nationalities?
- What is their religion?
- What do they look like?
- Do I look like them?

The drive within compelled me to keep searching until I found the answers. After spending many years corresponding with the Pinkerton investigators, search groups and agencies, and being disappointed repeatedly, I felt a strong urge to go to Goldsboro, North Carolina, where my relatives, the Weils, had lived, and where I had been told there might be a connection to my adoption. I also wanted to see Georgia McTier, who worked for the Weils. I kept in touch with her each Christmas over the years, and I felt she might know something about my adoption. Family servants seem to know many secrets, and I was hopeful.

Georgia McTier, age 107. Greensboro, North Carolina, 1982.

My friend, Anne Overstreet, went with me. As we drove into Goldsboro from the airport, we passed a sign that pointed to Patetown down a country road. "Look! Patetown!" I shouted excitedly. "Could that have any bearing on my name?"

"We haven't time to investigate now," Anne answered. "It's getting late, and we must drive to Greensboro to see Georgia." Georgia lived in the same old, white frame house in which she was born. Her "Auntie" took care of her. There she stood in the open doorway wearing a net cap secured tightly over her balding head. Although I knew she must be over 100 years old, she was still spry and I recognized her immediately. It was wonderful to see her again, but so sad to know that she could not see me, for she was blind. We hugged and kissed each other. She showed me the many photographs of the Weil and Sanger families hanging on her bedroom wall. Even though she could not see them, she knew each one by heart. We searched through old photograph albums and found snapshots of Ruthie and me taken in Goldsboro and in Toledo when we were children. These brought back happy memories.

Georgia had invited Hilda Weil Wallerstein, who remembered me as a child, to join us. Hilda was Uncle Lee's relative who once lived in Goldsboro but had moved to Greensboro. She looked in on Georgia periodically. "Did you know any Pates in Goldsboro?" I questioned Hilda.

"I knew Ezra Pate, a classmate of mine. It was years ago. He lived in the lowlands near your Aunt Ruth's and Uncle Lee's house. Why not call him?" she suggested. Was he related to me? I wondered.

Looking at Georgia with curiosity, I asked, "Georgia, how old are you now?"

"I gives 107," she replied proudly.

"Do you remember anything about my adoption?" "Oh Lawsie, yes!" she said, and this is what she told me:

"Mis' Ruth and Mista' Lionel lived in Goldsboro when they was first married. I started to work for them when I was very young. They wanted to have many chill'uns. After they had little Mista' Lee, Jr. and little Mis' Helen Marie, they tried to have more chill'uns, but no more came. I heard that they had arranged to adopt a baby. Two months before the baby was due, Mis' Ruth became pregnant. Oh, Lawsie, she didn't know what to do. She didn't want two babies so close together. So, she decided to tell her sister, Mis' Margaret, who lived in Toledo about the sits'iation. She knew that

Mis' Margaret wanted a baby real bad. Since all of the arrangements had been made, Mis' Margaret and Mista' Sig agreed to look into the adoption case. The baby was due to be born in February and Mis' Ruth's baby was due to be born the following September."

"Oh, Georgia, was that baby really me? Was she, Julia Pate, born February 3, 1924 in Greenville, South Carolina?" I could hardly contain myself with excitement. "Can you remember any more?"

"I heard," Georgia continued, "that the young girl came from a large farm family near Goldsboro and that they was too poor to take care of another baby. This young girl was sent to Greenville, South Carolina, in secrecy, to have her baby because she was not married."

This seemed to make sense to me, and I thought this must have been the reason my mother had traveled so far to adopt a child. After all, the arrangements had been made in advance.

I knew my father did not accompany my mother because he had sent a telegram of warning, which years later I found pasted in my baby book. It was sent on March 10, 1924, to 201 West Washington Street, Greenville, South Carolina, evidently where my mother had been staying. Did she manage this feat by herself, or did she have someone help her? Perhaps it was Miss Alice Ward, a district nurse, of whom she often spoke so fondly, who was by her side. The telegram read:

"To Mrs. Sigmond Sanger. If you have told your mother what Uncle Herman, myself and others think about early age, you may do what your joint judgements decide. You cannot experiment nor allow sentiment to govern. You must see it clearly and have no doubts. Opportunity will present itself without number. Weather very cold. Snow blizzard. Much love to all and to you dearest. SS."

From the many articles I had read, I learned that a happy ending to adopting a baby depended on several things: sound information, good judgment, patience and determination. Was this the warning my father was trying to convey to my mother in his telegram?

In today's world, with the advent of open adoption, in which birth mothers and adoptive parents have the opportunity to learn about each other, birth mothers are able to select adoptive parents based on their backgrounds. Perhaps my adoption, which I have surmised to have been private, was this kind of a selective agreement; first between the Weils and then the Sangers, knowing that a stable home and loving hearts would be offered by them to a child.

Another factor which reflects the changing face of adoption around the country since the time of my birth, is that birth mothers now are reluctant to put their babies up for adoption, either through agencies or by private adoption procedures. They are choosing to keep their babies and are raising them as single parents. Therefore, the number of waiting adoptive parents continues to grow. In retrospect, I think about the emotional strain my two "mothers" must have endured after my birth. One gave me life, the other perpetuated it.

There were still many unanswered questions. Who was this young unwed mother? Was she from Patetown? "Can you remember any more, Georgia?" I asked. "Your Mama, Mis' Margaret, took you first to Goldsboro to show you to the Weil family. I held you in my arms all night so that you wouldn't cry. No one was supposed to know that a baby was in the house. An adoption was 'hush-hush' back in those days. The next day I went to Baltimore with you and your Mama to help her board the B & O Railroad train bound for Toledo, where you was to meet your Papa. You was seven weeks old. Your cousin, little Mis' Ruthie, was born six months later on September 26, 1924."

"But Georgia, do you know what my birth mother's name was? Can you remember?"

"There were lots of Pates in Goldsboro. I remember that," she said. Then she squinted her eyes, thought hard and uttered, "I think her name was Annie." Annie Pate, is that really my birth mother's name? After all those years could Georgia actually remember? At least it was a clue, and I was hopeful again.

Chapter Sixteen
Southern Hospitality

*R*eturning to Toledo with an extra beat in my heart, I could hardly wait to proceed with my search. Georgia had given me what she thought was my birth mother's name, Annie Pate. But could I be sure? Georgia was 107 years old, so how could I rely on her memory? My heart sank at the thought.

In April, remembering Hilda Weil Wallerstein's suggestion, I telephoned Ezra Pate in Goldsboro. He couldn't have been nicer. After hearing my story, he referred me to his sister, Mrs. Ruth Pate Killette, who was doing a study of genealogy for the Pate family. Mrs. Killette referred me to her niece, Joyce Pate Herring, who she thought could be of help. When I telephoned her early in May, she was delighted to hear from a potential family member, and enthusiastically invited me to attend a Pate reunion in June. I could feel the warmth in her voice exuding that familiar Southern hospitality which convinced me to fly back to Goldsboro. I have always felt drawn toward Southerners.

Maybe it was my exposure to the South as a child or maybe it is just their charming way. My friend, Anne, is from Frankfort, Kentucky, and my roommate in boarding school and college, Evalina Brown Spencer, from Birmingham, Alabama.

That spring, Evalina and her husband, Bill, invited me to spend a few days with them. I planned to ask their advice and possible help with my search. When I told them I was seeking a copy of my original birth certificate in order to learn my birth mother's name, Bill suggested I contact his cousin, Tom Evins, a lawyer in Spartanburg, South Carolina, not far from Greenville. He thought his cousin might be able to help me get a court order which would enable me to obtain the information I needed. It sounded too good to be true. I telephoned Mr. Evins in Spartanburg and synchronized our appointment around the Pate reunion date, which was to be held in Goldsboro in June. My daughter, Mimi, accompanied me. There were no lawyers in Mimi's firm with licenses to practice in the state of South Carolina, but Mimi was anxious to be of help, and I was happy to have her support.

In his Southern drawl, Mr. Evins explained that one has to establish "good cause" in order to obtain a court order to open sealed records in South Carolina.

"Do you need to know because of health or financial problems?" he asked.

"No," was my honest answer.

"Curiosity or the desire to learn of one's identity is not 'good cause.' I am sorry but I cannot help you." He was a true Southern gentleman, but his charming manner did not help to lift my spirits.

The next day, Mimi and I drove to Goldsboro, North Carolina, to attend the Pate reunion. As we entered the large hall containing long banquet-style tables, I glanced around the room for resemblances, but found none. I felt at a loss and was confused. Who are all of these strangers named Pate? Am I related to them? Will anyone have an inkling about my background? Joyce Pate Herring greeted us with a warm, friendly smile, and immediately we felt welcomed. Recognizing my quandry, she was extremely kind and helpful by suggesting names of other Pate connections. She also referred us to the newspaper editor, the Wayne County Historical Society Room in the Goldsboro Library and the mortuary. We inquired at all of these places, but found no listings for Annie or Julia Pate.

Joyce then suggested we visit the old Deans Cemetery, where many Pates were buried. It was a small, fenced in cemetery nearly hidden from view on the hillside of a winding road leading to Patetown. Mimi and I climbed up

My birth mother's grave stone. Addie Pate Marsh, 1905-1942.

the stone steps leading to the rusty wrought iron gate, cautiously pushing aside tall weeds and underbrush, as we stepped inside. Walking past the weathered stone grave markers, we searched for Annie Pate's name. We copied all names, initials "A. P." and dates we thought pertinent, but did not find Annie's marker. As we were leaving, I spied one marker for Addie Pate Marsh, August 11, 1905, to December 23, 1942. I took note of this name because of the similarity to Annie, and the fact that she would have been nineteen years old at the time of my birth. But since we were looking for Annie, I did not give it any further thought. Together we carefully descended the slope to the road below, and returned to our waiting car. Before leaving Goldsboro, Joyce suggested we talk to Herman Pate, who was the manager of the Esso Gas Station near the old Weil house. When I told him about my search, he referred me to Charlotte Carrére, a genealogist living in Goldsboro. He thought she could help me.

Chapter Seventeen
I Couldn't Give Up Hope —Not Yet!

𝒰pon our return to Toledo, after so many well-meaning suggestions and what I felt was an unsuccessful trip, I telephoned Charlotte Carrére. She told me not to give up hope, as she had helped many people trace their roots. We began corresponding by mail and telephone. She searched in Goldsboro and I in Toledo.

My sister-in-law, Sally Swigart Krueger, who was also interested in genealogy, offered to help me. We searched for records in the Lucas County Court House, library articles, newspaper clippings, morgue and obituary records, Public Health Department records, Lucas County Children's Home records and finally the U.S. Census. The Mormon Tabernacle Temple in Salt Lake City, Utah, has complete records of all of the U.S. Census names which were accessible to me through the Genealogy Library of the Jesus Christ of Latter Day Saints Church in Toledo. We pored over hundreds of microfilms of Pate names. Sally and I also drove to the Fort Wayne, Indiana, library to search in the census and genealogy department. No pertinent information for Annie or Julia Pate was found.

By now, I was becoming obsessed with the idea of finding my identity. Other adoptees had been successful. Why wasn't I? I had put so much time and effort into my search that I couldn't give up –not yet!

Chapter Eighteen
A Genealogist, A Deputy Registrar and a Psychic

I decided to go back to Goldsboro and Greensboro, North Carolina, and to Greenville, South Carolina, to search more thoroughly. I wanted to meet Charlotte Carrére in person and to see Georgia again. In June, 1983, Sally accompanied me, and we flew to Goldsboro.

Our first stop was in Greensboro to see Georgia. I had hoped she could divulge more information about my adoption, but she could not. She did show us, however, that she could dance a jig. In her bedroom, she had strung a long cord from one end of the room to the other. As she turned on the radio, she hung on to the cord with both hands and swayed back and forth to the music. She was amazing! I never saw her again. She died at the age of 112, but she will live eternally in my memory.

From Greensboro we drove to

Goldsboro for a prearranged lunch with Charlotte. I looked forward to meeting the genealogist who had been helping to search in Wayne County, North Carolina. We exchanged our findings to date and became friends.

Sally and I then drove to Greenville, South Carolina, where we spent several days diligently searching through the records of children's agencies, city directories and hospital files. We were told the medical records belonging to Dr. L. W. Boggs, the doctor whose name appeared on my 1948 amended birth certificate, had been destroyed in a fire. Since Dr. Boggs was deceased, another avenue was closed to me. More disappointments and no leads were becoming a familiar pattern. I made an appointment to see Mary Crandall, a woman in Greenville who was connected with Adoptees and Birthparents in Search and with whom I had been corresponding. She suggested we go to the County Health Department to apply for my original birth certificate.

"There you will be given a form to fill out," she explained. Then firmly instructed, "Sign your name Julia Pate."

I was apprehensive about doing this, thinking it to be illegal; but after all, that was my name! When we arrived at the department, I did as she suggested. There was also a blank space for my birth mother's name. I filled in Annie Pate; father: unknown; date of birth: February 3, 1924; place of birth: Greenville, South Carolina, and nervously handed back this information through the window to the waiting clerk. She disappeared, and we waited anxiously. When she returned, she eyed me suspiciously and asked me to step into the back office. I entered, with Sally following close behind. My heart was pounding. As I faced the Deputy Registrar, Katherine Berry, sitting behind her desk, I thought: I have signed my name, Julia Pate, illegally, and now I am going to be arrested. Ms. Berry spoke,

"This is an adoption case, is it not?" I had to admit that it was, and my heart sank.

"How did you know your birth name and your birth mother's name?" she asked. I explained my story. "All of the information that you have stated on your application seems correct," she informed me, "as this is recorded in our old County Court House Record Book. However, I cannot give you a copy of your original birth certificate because it is a sealed record and probably recorded at the Department of Health and Vital Records in Columbia, South Carolina. I can only issue you a delayed birth certificate," she said.

As I examined this delayed birth certificate, I realized the information on it was taken from the first amended birth certificate my mother had given to me when I was twenty-four years old. The file date read May 27, 1948. The new delayed birth certificate was issued to me on June 20, 1983, and signed Katherine Berry, Deputy Registrar. I thanked Ms. Berry, was grateful I had not broken the law and quickly walked out with Sally.

Now I had two amended birth certificates, but not my original one. What to do? Should I go to Columbia, South Carolina? It seemed hopeless. Instead, Sally and I headed toward Asheville, North Carolina. My oldest friend in Toledo, Bill Skutch, suggested we visit Greta Smolowe, a woman who helped him during his illness through her psychic powers. She claimed to be in touch with celestial beings. Before we left Toledo, Bill arranged for us to meet with her.

As it was in a beautiful part of the Carolinas and we were feeling adventuresome, Sally and I drove through the mountains to Asheville and up Rabbit Skin Road to Greta's hilltop home. It was a spectacular setting, above the mist and clouds. Her house was equipped for protection against world disasters, such as acid rain and atomic bombs. Vegetable gardens and farm animals surrounded this self-sufficient spot for Greta and her family.

We spent a delightful few hours there. After listening to my story and learning about my quest to know my birth mother's name (I did not mention Annie Pate for fear of influencing her), Greta asked me, "Does the name 'Margot' mean anything to you?" I was startled!

"Of course," I said, "that was my adoptive mother's name." It sent shivers up and down my spine. How did she know? Why did she ask about her? I only wanted to know my birth mother's name. Then she continued, "I can't get past Margot. She says you're not to know." I was dumbfounded. I had waited all these years so as not to hurt her or anyone in the family before beginning the search for my identity. Now I hear I am not to know! Well, I had come this far, and I could not let this stop me now. I must continue with my search.

Chapter Nineteen
Is "Annie" Really Her Name?

$\mathcal{S}$ally and I returned to Toledo. It was August, 1983, and I still did not have any concrete information about my identity. Sometimes I felt it was useless to go on searching. Other times I had the urge to continue. After all, I thought I knew my birth mother's name, Annie Pate! Why is it so hard to locate her? Is that really her name?

I was in constant contact with Charlotte Carrére, who was still searching in North Carolina without success. Mimi, acting as my attorney, wrote letters to schools in both of the Carolinas seeking information about a student, Annie Pate, but to no avail. My doctor, Peter Overstreet, sent letters to hospitals in Greenville, South Carolina, requesting the medical records for Annie Pate and received negative replies. Joyce Pate Herring sent me names and information about many Pate families around Goldsboro. One name in particular she thought might be helpful to know was Clara Pate Garris, but this seemed doubtful to me at the time. I checked with the Lucas County Children's

75

home in Toledo asking for the records of Julia Pate (1924-1927) and was told there were none. I was at a standstill.

Then, in October, I wrote to the Department of Health and Vital Records in Columbia, South Carolina, where Katherine Berry, the Deputy Registrar at the Department of Health in Greenville, South Carolina, had mentioned that my original birth certificate was recorded, and requested a copy. I received a letter stating they had no record to send to me. I was not surprised. I had become immune to refusal letters. Again I telephoned Mary Crandall in Greenville, South Carolina, to ask her to follow-up in the search for my original birth certificate, after having explained about my two unsuccessful attempts at the Departments of Health and Vital Records in both Greenville and Columbia. She contacted her friend, Karen Connor, of Adoptees and Birthparents in Search in Columbia, relaying my story. In November, Karen telephoned me, and I explained my desperate situation.

"Why don't you write to the Department of Health in Greenville, South Carolina, and ask only for the information that is recorded in their old County Court House Record Book for Julia Pate, born February 3, 1924?" she suggested.

"What good will that do?" I asked. "I've already been there, filled out the application requesting my original birth certificate, and was given no more additional information." "I know," she said, "but this time do not ask for your original birth certificate." I wrote the letter half-heartedly, because I did not want to face another disappointment. The day before Thanksgiving of '83, I received an envelope addressed to me from the Department of Health and Environmental Control in Greenville, South Carolina. I was afraid to look inside for fear of another rejection. Apprehensively I tore the flap and opened the letter. It read:

"To whom it may concern:

The following information was recorded in the Greenville County Clerk of Court Birth Ledger, which is now in the custody of the Greenville County Health Department, provided by Section 44-63-200 of South Carolina Code of Laws, as amended.

Name: Julia Rowena Pate

Date of Birth: February 3, 1924

Mother's Maiden Name: Addie Pate

Place of Birth: Greenville County, South Carolina. These ledgers have been in the custody of the Greenville County Health Department since 1958. The date the information was recorded in the ledger is not known.

(Signed) Katherine Berry, Deputy County Registrar"

My heart was thumping and my hands were trembling as I stared in disbelief at the letter. There was my full name and my birth mother's name, "Addie"! How near this was to Annie, the name I had been searching for and believed to have been my birth mother's, the name Georgia had given me. She had tried so hard to remember and had come so close. Bless her heart! Then, there was Katherine Berry's signature, the woman with whom I had spoken in her office in Greenville. Did she remember me? Did she really want to help me, but could not give me this information because I had been applying for my original birth certificate?

My family was ecstatic upon hearing the news! This was the first step to my identity. The next was to learn about Addie Pate.

Chapter Twenty
"I Just Talked With My Sisters!"

After Thanksgiving, I telephoned Charlotte Carrére to relate the good news and the contents of my letter. I reminded her I had recorded a grave marker in the old Deans Cemetery for Addie Pate Marsh, born December 11, 1905, died December 23, 1942. "Could she have been my birth mother?" I asked. Charlotte immediately began to search for Addie's birth, death and marriage records in the Wayne County Court House, North Carolina. She telephoned me with her findings.

"Addie Ernestine Pate married Henry J. Marsh on February 26, 1927, in the parsonage of St. Paul's Methodist Episcopal Church in Goldsboro. She was twenty-two years old and Henry was thirty-one. The marriage license was signed by D. W. Pate and E. A. Pate. J. Henry Garris signed as witness."

Who are these people? Then, I recalled the name Joyce had sent to me as a possible lead and asked Charlotte, "Do you think there is a connection between the witness' signature and Clara Pate Garris' name?"

"I'll find out and let you know," she replied.

Suddenly, it dawned on me! It was two weeks after Addie's marriage (when I was three years old) that I was legally adopted. Addie and her husband must have felt the time had come to relinquish me to the Sangers. This explained the three-year gap in my young life, and why I had been legally held a ward of the Lucas County Children's Home in Toledo.

A few days later, both Charlotte and Joyce contacted Clara. It was a difficult task to approach a stranger with a story such as mine, and I was grateful for their attempt.

"Indeed, I knew Addie. We were double first cousins, and we were very close," Clara told them. "What a strange phenomenon this is! Just recently I had a dream about a baby. I was holding the baby in my arms and wondering to whom and where it belonged. Could this have been Addie's baby? You say the lady in Toledo is searching for her identity?" Clara was shocked.

There were others in Goldsboro to be contacted at Clara's suggestion: Audrey Garris Smith (Clara's daughter) and Shirley Thornton Warren (Audrey's cousin). When the story of my search was told to them, both women were helpful in supplying information to Charlotte and Joyce. It was Joyce who telephoned me first.

"Mar'Rooth," she drawled, "I have good news! You have two half-sisters; Waudelle Strickley in Grand Prairie, Texas, and Lauretta Dixon in Mechanicsville, Virginia."

I couldn't believe what I was hearing. Questions raced through my mind. What are they like? How old are they? Do I look like them?

"How did you find out?" I asked. "It's too wonderful to imagine." I was elated! Then, I added, "Maybe they don't want to know about me. What should I do?"

Joyce suggested I telephone Audrey and Shirley to

ask their advice. My heart was thumping when I called each one and introduced myself. My first question was: "Should I contact my sisters?"

"Of course," both replied. "Your sisters already know." They already know? How could that be? This was their story:

Addie's sister, Inez Pate Thornton, was Shirley's mother. The two sisters, Addie and Inez, were very close; therefore, Inez knew about Addie's pregnancy and knew she planned to put her baby up for adoption. After the baby was born, Addie cried a great deal, and said she was very concerned about the baby's whereabouts. Shirley's little sister, Mary, overheard her mother and Addie talking in the kitchen one day. "I want to find my baby," Addie sobbed. Inez told her softly but firmly, "That isn't a good idea. Such a discovery might disrupt the child's life, and you wouldn't want that to happen, would you?"

Long after Addie's death, Inez became ill. Before she died, she gathered Addie's two daughters, Waudelle and Lauretta, around her bedside and told them about a baby to whom their mother had given birth three years before she had married their father. "I do not know anything about the child nor where the child lives," she said. "I only know the baby was adopted. I wanted you both to hear the story, should you find out later in life and become shocked." What a coincidence it was that this occurred about the time I began to search for my identity!

I wondered if my two half-sisters took this news as casually as I did when I was told about being adopted. While I pondered the possibility of having siblings, were they inquisitive about the child? Aunt Inez prepared Addie's daughters well for such an occasion as this, for which I am thankful. Summing up all my courage, I went to the phone in my studio, surrounded by the mass of materials collected throughout my ten-year search. With fear and trepidation I dialed Lauretta's number in Virginia. "Lauretta? It's Mary Ruth, your sister from Ohio" . . . . "Yes, here I am!" I exclaimed. We jabbered furiously at great length before hanging up. Trembling with excitement, I immediately called Waudelle in Texas, and found myself gabbing happily with my other sister. Having just talked with each of my half-sisters, I was overcome with joy and thrilled with the expectation of meeting them. Because it was December, 1983, and nearly Christmas, we decided to organize a Pate reunion in Goldsboro on my sixtieth birthday, February 3, 1984. It would be a perfect way in which to celebrate. Suddenly I heard the front door open and shut.

"Yoo-hoo! Honey, I'm home!" called Tom. I flew down the stairs to greet him. "Hey, what's the matter? You look different. You're shaking all over," he said, grabbing my shoulders to steady me. Grinning, I blurted out, "I've just talked with my sisters!"

Part Three

The Pate Reunion

Chapter Twenty-one
My Ten Year Search Ends

$\mathcal{T}$he ten year search for my identity had come to an end. The Christmas holidays were over. A new year, 1984, was beginning, and I was going to North Carolina to meet my two half-sisters. I was bubbling with excitement and questions. What do they look like? Will they bring pictures of Addie? The month-long wait until my birthday seemed endless.

Preparations for the reunion began to unfold. Arrangements were made both in Toledo and Goldsboro, and the telephone lines were buzzing. What would I take? Photographs and an outline of my life seemed appropriate. Of course, Tom and our four children would accompany me.

"Mar'Rooth?" It was Joyce who telephoned. "Paul and I want to give a dinner party in our home on Friday evening for the immediate Pate families, so y'all can get to know each other before the big reunion on Saturday."

"That is so very thoughtful," I replied. "You have been wonderful already, and now you want to do more. How will I ever be able to thank you?"

"You don't have to thank me. We all are so excited to meet you and your family. The reunion will be at Wilbur's Bar-B-Q on Saturday at noon, and we'll be expecting about one hundred Pates. It's all arranged, thanks to Audrey and Shirley."

"That's incredible!" I exclaimed.

"Will you be driving or flying? If you're flying, we would like to meet you at the airport."

I told her we planned to fly directly to Goldsboro in the Spartan Chemical Company plane and would be arriving late Friday afternoon. Our reservations had been made at the Holiday Inn for the weekend.

"Tom and I would like to give a small dinner on Saturday evening, including the immediate Pate families and those who have helped me find my family. Could you recommend a good restaurant where we could host this dinner?" I asked. "I would like to make arrangements as soon as possible."

"I'll arrange it for you. It will be so much easier. Just tell me what you'd like to serve for dinner and how many guests you plan to invite."

I will be grateful forever to this lovely, gracious woman who gave so much of herself in order to help me.

Chapter Twenty-two
I First Saw My Birth Mother's Face

*J*oyce told me that each family group at the Pate reunion would be introduced and would say a few words about themselves. I planned to read the outline of my life leading up to the search for my identity. Copies were made to pass around at the reunion. I also brought along a photograph album depicting my growth and development in chronological order. Pictures of my parents, children and grandchildren were included.

I took gifts to my half-sisters and to all those who helped with my search –deciding that picture frames would make perfect presents. In addition, Tom and I sent red roses to Joyce and Paul in appreciation for their dinner party on Friday evening.

All through December and January, I received letters from my newfound relatives welcoming me into the Pate family. Lauretta, Waudelle and I exchanged family photographs. Then Lauretta sent me a picture of Addie. Was it a coincidence this arrived on December 23, the day Addie died, forty-two years previously? The thought sent chills through me. I held the photograph with both hands for fear of dropping it, and stared numbly at my birth mother's face. She was smiling and wearing a beret perched on her head and cocked jauntily to one side, similar to the one I wore thirty years later. I never tired of looking at her. I wondered how she and my father had met. How long had they known each other? Why didn't they marry? Who is he, and will I find him someday? Is he alive? Does he know about me? It was a few weeks later that I received the news from Lauretta that my father's name was Jacob (Jake) Calvin Sasser from Patetown.

Eva Pate Lancaster wrote to inform me that we were double cousins. Eva's father was Guy Pate, Addie's first cousin, and her mother was Nora Sasser, Jake's sister. All were deceased, including my father. Eva's birthday was February 25, 1924, making us only a few weeks apart in age. This was also Tom's and my wedding date, making it a double coincidence.

Jake's widow, Lillie Mae Hare Sasser, still lived in Patetown and knew Eva. Having been told about the discovery of my identity, she became very upset. She did not know her husband had fathered an illegitimate daughter.

"I don't want to meet her and don't want my son, Jack, to learn about her," she confided to Eva. Of course, I was disappointed, but I wanted to respect her wishes. This was the only negative response to my search of which I was aware. I could understand how shocked she must have been to learn of my existence. It was exciting news for me, however, to learn that I had a half-brother, and I felt someday I would meet him.

My birth mother, Addie Pate Marsh. Richmond, VA. Age 28, 1933.

My resem- blance to my birth mother. Age 39, 1963.

Chapter Twenty-three
Meeting My Two Half-Sisters for the First Time

$\mathcal{I}$t was February 2, 1984, the day of our departure for Goldsboro. With everything in order and cameras in hand, we climbed aboard the Spartan King-Air. There were just enough seats to hold the six of us and the pilot. Tom flew co-pilot, and our children and I sat in the back. The tension mounted as we neared Goldsboro. Will Joyce and Paul be there to meet us? When will

The Holiday Inn, Goldsboro, North Carolina. February 2, 1984.

I see my sisters? Will we like each other? I was beginning to wonder if I had made the right decision to search for my identity. But, it was too late now. We were about to land.

Circling the field, I could see people waving. Joyce and Paul greeted us warmly. I was beaming as introductions took place. Because they surrounded us with such genuine Southern hospitality, I felt as if we were already long-time friends.

Arriving at the Holiday Inn, my children shouted, "Hey, Mom! Look at the Holiday Inn sign. There's your name on the marquee." It read, "Happy Birthday Mary Ruth."

I laughed and said, "I've always wanted my name in lights –just like Grandma." Who was responsible for this delightful surprise? I wondered.

As we scrambled out of our car, Meg turned to look at a car that had just pulled up behind us. "There's your sister, Mom," she said. "I can tell because she looks so much like you. Your noses are the same."

I turned around nervously to look. As the woman stepped out of her car, I noticed she was taller than I, had a reddish cast to her hair and had high cheekbones. Then I recognized her from her photographs. "Lauretta, is that you?" I called out. We rushed toward each other. It felt awkward, but good, to embrace a sister I had never known. We stood smiling and peering into each other's faces seeking our resemblances. Her husband Bill, their two sons, William and John, and their daughter, Joanne (with beautiful red hair) were with them.

After introducing our families, Lauretta said, "Waudelle, her husband, Ben, and five of their seven children, Bonita, Karen, Debbie, David and Mike (twins), plus Mike's fiance, Sherri, have already checked into the Holiday Inn. Come on! Let's go to their rooms so y'all can meet." She led the way.

There I was standing face-to-face with my other half-sister, Waudelle. Trembling with excitement, I hugged her. She was about my height and wore tinted glasses. While her face was rounder than Lauretta's, she had high cheekbones too. She did not have red hair, but medium brown hair like mine. Did I look like either sister? Having had the same mother, but not the same father, made it hard to tell. Since I had grown up with no one who looked like me, I always searched for resemblances. My head was whirling with questions.

"This is wonderful," I exclaimed. "I can't believe this really is happening. Here we are together in Goldsboro, where it all began."

All of our assorted children retired to the Holiday Inn lounge to become acquainted, leaving us to do the same in Waudelle's and Ben's room.

"How about a drink?" suggested Tom. "This calls for a celebration." Wayne was a dry county, but we all had thought to take along a little fortification to steady our nerves. We laughed at having had the same idea and proposed a toast to our first meeting.

"Tell me everything," I began. "Did you bring photographs? Are there more of Addie?" I could not bring myself to call Addie "Mother." I had known only one mother who had raised and loved me, and she would always be my mother.

We sat down on the beds and began the game of "Show and Tell." Besides some photographs of Addie with Waudelle and Lauretta as children, their father, Henry Marsh, and Addie and Henry's wedding picture, Lauretta very carefully unwrapped a package. It was a piece of Addie's hair.

"Mother's hair was long, thick and wavy and she usually braided it around her head," said Waudelle. The color was chestnut brown, similar to mine as a child. An eerie sensation flowed through me as I stroked

93

my birth mother's silky locks. Tears welled up in my eyes. I could not speak, but my thoughts were of how much I would have liked to have known her.

I brought out the photograph of Addie in her saucy beret. As I gazed again at her smiling face and then at

With my half-sisters, Lauretta Dixon
and Waudelle Strickley.
February 2, 1984.

my two sisters, suddenly it came to me: There it was! Addie's smile! We all had her broad smile. At last I found a resemblance that belonged to me, and I was thrilled.

Longing to know more about Addie, I questioned my sisters further. "We were quite young when Mother died, but I know she loved to sew and made many of our clothes," Waudelle told me.

"I remember a powder blue velvet coat with a matching cap mother made for me," Lauretta said. "I seemed to be wearing it in many photographs." She went on to say, "We were told that when rummaging through her belongings, soon after her death, a set of dried-up water color paints was found with some old brushes in a box at the bottom of a chest of drawers. Nobody realized she liked to paint."

Joyce and Paul Herring, February 2, 1984. (above)

Clara Pate Garris at the piano. February 2, 1984. (below)

Had I inherited my birth mother's talent for painting? I was delighted at the thought.

That evening we drove to the Joyce and Paul's charming country home for dinner. Twenty-nine Pate relatives warmly greeted us. There were name tags for everyone, gifts were exchanged, Clara Pate Garris played the piano and cameras flashed at every opportunity. Because most of the Pates were Southern Baptists, non-alcoholic punch was served before the delicious buffet-style dinner. Joyce had baked two birthday cakes for dessert. It was a very special celebration, and my family and I were overcome with joy.

Chapter Twenty-four
A Sea of Unfamiliar Faces

*S*aturday, February 3, was my six-tieth birthday, and the day of the Pate re-union. My family and I arrived at Wilbur's Bar-B-Q to find one hundred and four Pates waiting to greet us. A sea of unfamiliar faces turned to look as we walked through the door. They were all seated at long tables covered with red and white checkered cloths. I smiled and heard someone say, "I could tell she was Addie's girl the minute she walked in."

The room was filled with the mouth-watering aroma of barbecued pork and all the trimmings, including mashed potatoes with gravy, corn on the cob, assorted salads and apple pie. After this delicious Southern-style meal, Joyce called the clan to order. She welcomed me and introduced each Pate family group, who, in turn, spoke briefly about their family members. Albert Pate read a report of the Pate genealogy, in which I learned that my great-great-great grandfather, Silas Pate, married an Indian maiden, curiously named Christian. Was

Meg, Mimi, Tommy, Steve, Mary Ruth and Tom.
The Swigart family at the Pate Reunion,
February 3, 1984.
Goldsboro, North Carolina.

this the source of my high cheekbones and our baby grandson's looks? Incredible! I thought.

I was the last to speak. I introduced my family, and then read the prepared outline of my search. My photograph album was passed around from table to table, along with copies of my speech. If I had any doubts about finding my roots, I knew then I needn't have worried. Nearly everyone was staring happily at me after confirming I looked like a Pate. I had come full circle, Goldsboro to Goldsboro, and felt as if I belonged.

Selah Ann Edmundson Pate Steven at the Pate Reunion, February 3, 1984.

"I am so lucky," I commented.

"No, you're not lucky!" responded Aunt Ruth Pate Killette from her wheelchair. "You are only lucky when others lose. Those who lose are like Lucifer the Devil. Others are blessed. You are blessed!"

Ruth Pate Killette at the Pate Reunion, February 3, 1984.

Chapter Twenty-five
A Memorable Birthday

$\mathcal{S}$aturday evening, our family hosted the dinner party for my immediate newfound family and for those who had been so helpful to me throughout the years of my search. Joyce had made the arrangements at Jenning's Seafood and Steak Restaurant. There were thirty of us, including my genealogist, Charlotte Carrére, my double cousin, Eva Pate Lancaster, and her son, Martin, who was a North Carolina State Representative.

Audrey Garris Smith and Shirley Thornton Warren, February 3, 1984.

Two years later he was to become the Democratic U.S. Congressman from the 3rd District of North Carolina.

As we entered the private dining room, I spied more presents and another birthday cake. It was to be a second celebration. One gift was a beautiful ceramic tobacco leaf jar. Eva gave me a tiny carving Jake had made from a peach stone. "He loved to whittle, and I thought you would like to have this." I was thrilled to have something made by my father. We hugged, we kissed, and we cried with joy. To thank them all adequately for their generosity and thoughtfulness was near to impossible.

"This is the most wonderful birthday I could have, being able to bring together my immediate family and my recently discovered Pate family." I began. "Having come to the end of a ten-year search for my identity and finding so much warmth, receptiveness and love among 'y'all', makes me glow from within with happiness. A feeling of belonging fills my heart at seeing photographs of Addie and recognizing our resemblance to each other."

I couldn't help but wonder what my adoptive parents, the Sangers, and my Aunt Ruth and Uncle Lee Weil would have thought of my success. I hoped they would have approved of my search.

"In celebration of this special occasion," I added, "would 'y'all' like to join with me in singing the North Carolina Tar Heel Song? I learned it years ago from my cousin, Lee Weil, Jr."

> "'I'm a Tar Heel born,
> I'm a Tar Heel bred,
> And when I die,
> I'll be a Tar Heel dead.
> So, it's Rah-Rah Carolina 'lina,
> Rah-Rah Carolina 'lina,
> Rah-Rah Carolina, Rah-Rah-Rah!'"

With that, the evening ended on a high note!

Charlotte Carrére, my geneologist. February 3, 1984.

Eva Pate Lancaster and her son, Martin Lancaster; North Carolina State Representative. February 3, 1984.

Cora Lee Pate Beamon and her husband, Charles. February 3, 1984.

Singing "The Tar Heel Song",
February 3, 1984.

Sunday came and it was time to head back to Toledo. We all waved through the windows of the plane to those Pates who had come to the airport to say good-bye. As I gazed down at them and at the smiling faces of Tom and our children, I realized how truly blessed I was. I nestled down in my seat with happy thoughts of the most memorable birthday of my life. Having accomplished my mission, I was at peace. I had become a part of a new, warm, and receptive family.

Part Four

The Sasser Reunion

Chapter Twenty-six
I First Heard My Half-Brother's Voice

$\mathcal{L}$ate in February, Tom and I flew to the Dominican Republic to visit our friends, Annabel and Bill Custer, at their golf villa in the Casa de Campo Resort. We played golf, swam and indulged in the luxurious life. Tom had a chance to "stick and ball" with some top polo players before a polo match.

One evening in the middle of a card game, I was summoned to the telephone. "Who can it be?" I questioned worriedly. "I hope nothing is wrong at home," I said, glancing at Tom. My legs were shaking as I hurried to the phone and picked up the receiver.

"Hello, Mar' Rooth?" a Southern voice inquired. "This is your brother, Jack Sasser, from Smithfield, North Carolina. I hope I didn't scare you. I just learned that you are my sister."

"Oh, my! Jack!" I exclaimed. "I can't believe it's you! How did you find out about me?"

"My mother decided to tell me. I was so excited that I had to call you."

"How did you find me here?" I asked.

"It took a bit of doing to track you down, but I called Spartan Chemical Company in Toledo and was given your number in the Dominican Republic. When can we meet?" He sounded breathless, and so was I.

"We are flying to Nassau from here for a company meeting," I told him, "but we'll be back in Toledo in a few weeks and then I'll call you. I can't wait to meet you, Jack."

Rushing back to the card table, I exclaimed, "That was my brother, Jack. I can't believe it!" Tom gave me a happy squeeze and the others asked in unison, "How did he find you? What does he do? Does he have a family?"

I was too overcome with joy to answer them. More questions started spinning around in my head. Soon I would know the answers.

On February 25, Tom and I celebrated our fortieth wedding anniversary in Nassau, before the arrival of Spartan's ten top regional managers and their wives. After a successful few days of meetings, we returned to Toledo.

In early March, I contacted Charlotte Carrére, my genealogist in Goldsboro. Previously, I had told her that my father was Jacob Calvin Sasser from Patetown. Now, I could tell her I had spoken with my half-brother, Jack Hare Sasser, from Smithfield, North Carolina.

"That's wonderful," she said. "I can tell how happy you are."

"Did you find any information about my father 'Jake' Sasser?" I asked.

"I have been working on that and am sending you copies of his birth, marriage and death certificates."

I learned from her that Jake had been born on May 30, 1897, married Lillie Mae Hare on December 1, 1932, and died on July 5, 1952 at the age of fifty-five.

"By the way," she added, "did you know you are descended from the French Huguenots? They first settled in South Carolina in 1683 and later migrated to North Carolina. The name Sasser stems from the French name de Saussier," she informed me. It was astounding to discover my biological father's background was French. Since I had been exposed to the language most of my life, this delighted me. I knew there was much more to learn about my heritage.

Chapter Twenty-seven
Tom Becomes Ill

*I*n April, I flew to Cincinnati to attend an oil and pastel painting workshop instructed by the portrait artist, Daniel Greene. I stayed with Tom's cousin, Ruth Swigart, for the week. At the end of the session, Ruth hosted a dinner party and asked Tom to fly in from Toledo to join us.

Upon his arrival, I was shocked at his appearance and suspected that something was terribly wrong. He had never mentioned an ailment to me and had never complained about his health during our forty years of marriage. He admitted to not feeling up to par, and promised to call the doctor once we got home.

We flew home in time to spend Easter Sunday with our family. Late that afternoon, Tom telephoned our friend, Dr. Peter Overstreet, who lived a block away.

"Meet me at my office right away," Pete insisted. "I want to examine you and take some x-rays."

When Tom and Pete returned to the house together, Pete announced, "There is a shadow on Tom's lung."

I shuddered for fear of the worst.

The next day, Tom entered the hospital, and after myriad tests it was confirmed to be lung cancer. The lower lobe of his left lung was removed. After a long hospital stay, followed by radiation treatments, he spent the remainder of the summer recuperating at home, enjoying the companionship of his family, his dog and basking in the sun.

Chapter Twenty-eight
Meeting My Half-Brother
for the First Time

*M*y brother Jack was so anxious to meet me, that when Tom felt better, we arranged a visit in Toledo toward the end of June. "How will I know you, Jack?" I asked.

First meeting with my brother,
Jack Hare Sasser, Toledo, Ohio.
June 15, 1984.

"I'll be the one with a red rose."
Nervously, I waited at the airport for his

With Jack at the entrance to Spartan Chemical Company. June 16, 1984.

Tom, Jack and Steve on board the "Hidilution". June 16, 1984.

Jack and Judy Sasser with Bill Skutch, enjoying party held at the Barnum's home. June 16, 1984.

arrival. I first saw him when I looked up from the bottom of the escalator where I stood. He was riding down toward me holding a bunch of red roses in his arms. Through misty eyes, I could see that he was tall, good looking and had a shock of brown hair.

"Jack, is it really you?" We hugged, laughed and cried all at the same time. "Thank you for the beautiful roses," was all I could manage to say.

"This is Judy," he said, as he introduced his pretty wife. She was short with dark hair and had a bubbly personality. Immediately, we became friends.

"It is wonderful to have you both here," I exclaimed. "Tell me about your family."

"We have two children, Jay and Jacque, and we call ourselves the 'Four Js,'" they answered in unison. Then, Jack continued, "I have a degree in electrical engineering from North Carolina State University and work at Data General."

As their flight arrived late in the evening, we tip-toed into our house, so as not to disturb Tom's sleep, and waited until morning for introductions.

That day plans were made to tour Spartan Chemical Company in the morning, and to view Toledo's skyline by boat in the afternoon. Mother Nature provided perfect weather for our picnic cruise on board Spartan's fifty-three foot Hatteras, the Hidilution. It was a family get-together including our children; my sister-in-law, Sally; her husband, Wally Krueger; and their children. A beautiful party was given by some of our friends that evening in honor of Jack and Judy. It was a Southern cook-out at Jeane and Tony Barnum's country home. Tables covered with flowered cloths were set on the lawn leading to the quarry in front of their house, and Tony's private airplane hangar and runway could be seen in the distance. Overhanging trees reflecting in the quarry made a picturesque setting for this special event.

Jack in the "Great Lakes Trainer", ready for take-off. June 17, 1984.

The next morning, Tom, who was not yet well enough to fly himself, arranged for Jack and Judy to be flown in his Great Lakes Trainer, an open cockpit stunt bi-plane. With goggles and helmets in place, they took off. We watched them soaring in and out of the clouds, as the pilot, Jim Lenardson, maneuvered the plane through loops and lazy eights.

"That was an experience I'll never forget," Jack declared in a quivering voice as he tried to steady his wobbling legs. "I'm happy to be standing right-side-up again!"

Before Jack and Judy's departure, the Overstreets hosted a brunch at the Inverness Country Club. The weekend was full

A big hug at The Inverness Country Club. June 17, 1984.

of special memories, not only of my brother and his wife, but of how blessed I was to have such dear friends to help make it so.

Tom continued with his radiation treatments and soon seemed well enough to be able to take a short trip to Nantucket in August. We visited his cousins, Margie and Will Haley, and Anne and Gil Flues, both of whom lived in Washington, D.C. They had rented a quaint cottage near the sea for the month. It was delightful to be with them. Although Tom tired easily, he thoroughly enjoyed himself.

Chapter Twenty-nine
Planning a Pig Pickin'

*O*ver the summer my brother, Jack, and Eva Lancaster had been busy making plans for a Sasser reunion in Goldsboro, North Carolina. They were anxious to have me meet my Sasser relatives, and I was looking forward to meeting them.

"We want to have a pig-pickin'" Jack said over the phone. "You say when it's best for you to come."

We decided September would be a good month. Tom had finished his radiation treatments and seemed well enough to travel. He was as eager as I to meet the Sasser side of my family, since the Pate reunion in February had been so special and successful.

"How does your mother feel about this, Jack?" I questioned. "Is she willing to meet me now?"

I was worried, but Jack assured me she was ready. She had been told about me, my family, the Pate reunion, and about Jack and Judy's visit to Toledo. Now, she supposed it was time for us to meet.

Invitations were sent out with a picture on

the front of a baby yellow chick being hatched from a broken shell. Inside it read:

> "What's new?
> With a new chick in the family
> a reunion is due.
> Her name is Mary Ruth Swigart
> and she'd like to meet you.
> We've hatched up a gathering
> and a pig-pickin' for the taste.
> To make it complete,
> we need you in place.
> Please plan on September 29
> to be with us at five,
> At Stoney Creek FWB Church,
> where we'll celebrate that she's arrived."

Our son, Tommy, and my sister-in-law, Sally, joined us on the Spartan plane and, once more, we were off to Goldsboro.

Chapter Thirty
Lillie Mae

"It's wonderful to be here again." I said to Jack upon our arrival. "I'm looking forward to meeting all of the Sassers and especially your mother."

Joyce and Paul kindly loaned us one of their cars for the weekend. We followed Jack down the same country road where I had seen the sign pointing to Patetown on my first trip to North Carolina in 1982. This road also led to the old Deans Cemetery where Addie was buried. Having received genealogy charts of the Pate and Sasser families, I learned my maternal grandparents, Patience Land Donia Deans and Isadore Atlas Pate, had nine children, including Addie. My paternal grandparents, Bette E. Pilkington and Jackson Jensen Sasser had six children, including Jake. Both of these families had lived in this little community of Patetown, and had farmed the rich land on which tobacco, corn, soy beans and cotton were grown. Jack's mother, Lillie Mae, still lived in Patetown, in the same pale green, frame house in which she and Jake had raised their family. I was curious, yet nervous, about meeting her. What will she think of me?

She greeted us at the door, and immediately I realized I need not have worried. She was a tall, impressive woman with a graciousness and warmth about her which left me with no doubt that we would soon become friends. A delicious buffet with homemade lemon meringue pie awaited our arrival. Eva and Cora Lee Pate Beamon were also there to welcome us.

"I am truly glad that you completed your search, Mary Ruth," Lillie Mae said. "Jack was so excited when I told him about you. I wasn't sure how it would affect him to suddenly find he had a sister, so I hesitated in telling him when I first learned about you. Now I know I made the right decision." This relieved my anxiety and I smiled warmly at her. "As you know," she continued, "Jake and I had two sons, Richard Calvin Sasser and Jack Hare Sasser. Richard was only thirty-seven years old when he died in 1973. He had a brain tumor, which was caused by a fall when he was a young boy. Richard's widow, Margaret, and their four children live with me." Previously, Eva had sent me a photograph of Jake taken when he was a young man. As we walked into the living room, I saw other pictures of him on the mantel and the table. It was a modest and comfortable room with a large piano at the front window.

Lillie Mae and Jake Sasser's house.
Patetown, North Carolina.
September 29, 1984.

My biological father, Jacob Clavin Sasser (Jake),
with hand in pocket, standing next
to John R, Lancaster.c. 1920's.

My father, Jake, wearing bow tie, sitting next to Guy Pate, Eva Pate Lancaster's father. c. 1920's.

Jake's gas station and old Ford car. Patetown, North Carolina, 1929.

Being in my father's house, peering at his photographs and talking with my "step-mother," left me with an indescribable feeling. I stared at Jake's face and wished he were still alive. He had died of a heart attack in 1952, at the age of fifty-five.

As I held his picture, Lillie Mae said to me, "You know, Jake always wore a hat." I could see he had deep-set brown eyes and dark hair, both of which Jack and I have. He had a slight build and was not very tall. Is that why he always wore a hat—to make himself appear taller, I wondered?

Directly across the main road in front of Lillie Mae's house was a gas station and small store.

Margaret Pate Sasser,
Richard's widow, with children:
Jeff, Pate, Tim and Jeanie.
September 29, 1984.

"Jake was part owner of that establishment," Lillie Mae proudly informed us. "He also farmed."

Getting up, she asked, "Would you like to walk across the side road to the Free Will Baptist Church? The Sasser reunion will be held there this evening, but first I would like to show you something."

"Mother plays the piano every Sunday in the church,"

Jack said smiling at her. As we entered, Lillie Mae pointed with pride to a colorful painting which was recessed in the wall at the end of the sanctuary.

"This painting of the mouth of the River Jordon at the Sea of Galilee was given in memory of Jake," she informed us. It hung behind the altar with the baptistry three or four steps below and made an impressive sight. I tried to imagine my father and his family attending Sunday services in the sanctuary right where I was standing.

With Jack in front of Stoney Creek First
Will Baptist Church, Patetown,
North Carolina.
September 29, 1984.

Leaving the church, we walked to the cemetery directly to the left.

"This is where Jake and Richard are buried." We stopped to gaze at the two grave markers. They read:

Jacob C. Sasser - May 30, 1897 - July 5, 1952

Richard Calvin Sasser - Apr. 5, 1936 - Oct. 26, 1973.

It was extraordinary, I thought, to be here in Patetown where both my mother and father had lived and been buried. As if Lillie Mae had read my thoughts, she said:

"You know, I knew Addie years ago when we were young girls. She used to stop by to see me after Sunday school services. I always wondered why, because she was older, but we became friends. Now I know it was to see Jake, who lived nearby. They would meet at my house and go off together on Sunday afternoons giggling and holding hands. I was told a few years later she had been sent away to the Cullowhee School in South

My father's gravestone:
Jacob Calvin Sasser,
1897-1952.

My brother's gravestone:
Richard Calvin Sasser,
1936-1973.

Carolina. Then I heard she didn't like the school and returned home in February. Let's see now, you were born February 3, 1924, weren't you? Nobody knew she had given birth to a baby. So you can imagine how shocked I was to learn about you." Suddenly I realized that my birth might have been kept a secret even from my father. No wonder Lillie Mae was stunned and initially reluctant to meet me. My heart went out to her. Then she continued, "One day, a few years later, Jake knocked on my door. I said, "Addie isn't here." He surprised me by saying, "I'm not here to see Addie. I'm here to see you." Could he have had a crush on Lillie Mae all along? Then Lillie Mae smiled, and with a twinkle in her eye, she said, "We were married soon after that."

Chapter Thirty-one
Country Home Cookin'

*B*y five o'clock in the afternoon, we arrived at the Free Will Baptist Church for the Sasser Reunion and the pig-pickin'. Again, the familiar aroma of pork with all the trimmings filled the hall. Eva's husband, Harold Lancaster, had spent the day roasting the pig at his hideaway cabin in the country.

Watching Harold Lancaster roast the pig for the pig pickin'. Septmber 29, 1984.

Earlier that afternoon, we stopped by to view the cooking process. As we approached a clearing in the woods, we found ourselves drawn toward a smoky cloud emitting a delicious aroma of roasted pork. Harold stood by the grill, cap on his head, fork in one hand, hot pad in the other and lifted the cover. The pig was nearing completion. He offered us samples speared by the sharp pointed tines of his long fork. Nothing could have tasted better than those tender crispy pieces that melted in our mouths.

Jack with his mother, Lillie Mae Sasser, at the Sasser Reunion. September 29, 1984.

The Sasser reunion was as enjoyable as the Pate gathering. Everyone welcomed us with open arms. Delicious homemade casseroles, salads and desserts were brought for all to share. Of course, the pig was a special treat. I felt overcome with joy to have found these wonderful relatives and stood up to tell them so.

Jack and Judy invited us for breakfast the next morning. I was anxious to see their home and, since Smithfield was not far from Goldsboro, we ventured forth. A scrumptious array of home baked muffins, ham, eggs, fruit and coffee awaited us. Lillie Mae greeted us warmly.

Their modern ranch house overlooked a sloping, wooded backyard. To one side was a large play house Jack had built for Jacque. She also had a beautiful doll collection. Jacque loved to paint and was an accomplished acrobatic and ballet dancer. Jay was an active high school student.

We attended their church service at the First Baptist Church in Smithfield, before driving back to Goldsboro to have lunch with Judy's parents, Ida Bell and Grier Watkins. We found Grier churning homemade peach ice cream in the backyard.

"What a treat this has been," I said as I thanked them all. "The whole weekend has been special. We hate to leave right after such a delicious lunch, but it's time to fly back to Toledo."

With Tom, Tommy and Sally Swigart Krueger, my sister-in-law, at the Sasser Reunion. September 29, 1984.

Everyone, including Lillie Mae, Margaret and her family, Eva Lancaster, and the Herrings drove to the airport to bid us good-bye. Sadly, we waved to them all as we taxied down the runway.

It was a weekend packed full of memories. As we flew through the clouds, I realized how fortunate I was to have found my two extended families, the Pates and the Sassers. More than that, they were receptive

With Jack in front of Spartan Chemical Company's "King Air", ready for departure to Toledo. September 30, 1984.

and openly gave me their love. I learned what all my life I had longed to know: from whence I came and whom I resembled. I have my mother's smile and my father's deep-set brown eyes. I was happy and contented, and ready to go home.

My two sisters, Waudelle and Lauretta, and my brother, Jack, did not know one another. My next objective was to have them meet.

Chapter Thirty-two
Tom Succumbs to Lung Cancer

*T*om was very tired after the Sasser reunion. Ruth Swigart telephoned from Cincinnati to tell us about a new drug called Interferon which was thought to be a promising cure for cancer. "The M. D. Anderson Cancer and Tumor Clinic in Houston is the place to go for treatment," she informed us. After talking with Dr. Gutterman, head of the program, we became hopeful about this new medication. Plans were made to fly to Texas in October, 1984.

Because Tom was an outpatient, we lived at the Marriott Hotel which was close to the clinic where he took his daily treatments. We walked the two short blocks in the beginning of our stay. As the weeks passed he became weaker, so we took a taxi or asked the bellman at the hotel to drive us.

It amazed me to see how "upbeat" all of the doctors and nurses were. They displayed a great deal of optimism and offered encouragement to every patient. After a while, I became accustomed to the yellow pallor and bald heads of these courageous patients. I attended classes to learn how to give Tom his daily Interferon shots and to learn how to change his D.M.F.O. pump, which held his special medication for blood platelets. Every four hours, twenty-four hours a day, was the routine for pump changing. We arranged to be called by the hotel wake-up service during the night, for fear we would sleep through the four-hour interval. Although his pain had increased, he seldom complained, and we felt he was conquering his illness.

In November, I flew to El Paso, Texas, for a night's visit with my cousin, Ruth Weil Harris and her husband, Bill. I wanted to tell them about my search and to see for myself their reaction to it. I believe they were surprised I had undertaken such a project and, like most people, wondered why I had bothered to do it. However, they were enthusiastic about the outcome.

In December, I flew to Toledo for a few days to get ready for Christmas. Tom and I were anticipating going home for the holidays and then returning for further treatments in January. Between my two absences, our children and Spartan employees flew to Houston to visit with Tom.

"All I want to do is to go home, sit in the den, and pat my dog!" Tom said to me one day. I knew how he felt, and I desparately wished he could do just that.

December 14 was Tom's birthday. He was born in 1924, sixty years before, in his grandparents' house in North Baltimore, Ohio. He grew up in Toledo, where we met and raised our family. I ordered a surprise birthday cake and invited the kind and helpful hotel employees to join us in the celebration. Tom always loved to play the piano so we had one moved into our suite earlier in our stay. I asked him to play a tune for his birthday guests, but for the first time, he refused. "I just don't feel like it now." he said. It was not like him.

The next day my sister, Waudelle, who lived near

Dallas, was scheduled to visit for the weekend. She had been planning this trip since our arrival in Houston. I had not seen her since the first time we met at the Pate reunion nearly a year ago, and I was anxious to become better acquainted.

We spent Saturday afternoon at the new three-tiered shopping mall in downtown Houston. The Christmas display was magnificent and huge, as only to be expected in Texas. Christmas carols rang out from several choirs of "real" people precariously perched among the branches of the gigantic Christmas tree nearly reaching to the top of the mall. It was a spectacular sight and a beautiful performance.

Returning to the hotel, we found Tom listless and pale, with blood trickling from the corner of his mouth. Immediately I called the doctor who told me to disconnect his pump and take him to the emergency room at the clinic. We walked him to the elevator, helped him into a cab and hurriedly took him to the clinic. He was put into the intensive care unit where we learned he was bleeding internally. It was a blessing I had Waudelle for moral support.

After Tom had been made comfortable, we were told to return to the hotel to get some sleep. It was very late, so I kissed him good-night and said, "I love you, honey. I'll see you in the morning." He looked at me and smiled weakly.

At six o'clock a.m. the telephone rang, and I was informed that Tom was comatose.

"I'll change my early morning reservations to Dallas and stay with you," Waudelle offered.

"Bless you," I said. "It's a miracle you are here. God must have known to send you to me on this particular weekend." She stayed until my children and our family doctor, Peter Overstreet, arrived that afternoon.

Tom died five days later on December 20, 1984.

Tony Barnum and George Urschel, Jr., flew to Houston in one of Tony's planes to take his body back to Toledo. Through my grief and sorrow, I could not help but think how pleased Tom would have been to know that he and his friends were taking the last of their many flights together. Now, Tom was going home. My children and I flew to Toledo in the Spartan Company plane. I could never express my appreciation, gratitude and love to our wonderful friends for their help and support in my time of need.

When I walked into my house, to my surprise, there was my Christmas tree beautifully decorated. Tears streamed down my face. This thoughtful gesture from our special friends helped ease the pain of returning home to an empty house.

Tom was buried on December 23, not an easy time of the year for anyone. Our good friends, the Baileys, flew from Denver and my brother, Jack, Judy and their daughter Jacque, drove from Smithfield, North Carolina, for the funeral. I was deeply touched.

In that one year, I experienced many events, both happy and sad. Tom and I had celebrated our sixtieth birthdays and our fortieth wedding anniversary. I had found my two biological families, but I had lost my partner, my love, my husband. Was this God's will? What is my destiny?

I am a widow and must survive.

Part Five

Wassi

Chapter Thirty-three
Ham and Yam

*1*985 did not begin happily for me. I found myself in the midst of writing thank you letters for the many contributions given in Tom's memory, attending to business and personal matters and, in general, feeling sorry for myself. My life was busy, but lonely. I took comfort in my family, my friends and my devoted dog, Duke. Spring arrived and Jack and Judy telephoned. "There's going to be the annual Ham and Yam Festival in Smithfield, and we want you to come for a visit."

It sounded like fun and just what I needed; a change of pace from my endless drudgery. I gratefully accepted their invitation. It turned out to be a wonderful weekend. The morning of the festival we strolled down main street, passing booth after booth of country hams roasting to perfection on rotating spits, and emitting that delicious aroma with which I had become so familiar. There were arts and crafts displays and jazz bands, interspersed with hog calls and laughter. Jack and I were interviewed by a staff writer from the local newspaper. Our picture and a story entitled, "Her Search for Roots Turned Up Brother She Didn't Know She Had" appeared in the Smithfield Herald on April 30, 1985.

As I was still eager to learn more about my biological background, that afternoon Jack and Judy took me to visit Selah Ann Edmundson Pate Stevens, who lived in Lucama, not far from Smithfield. Selah Ann's first husband, Marvin Pate, was Addie's brother. Jack felt she could enlighten me with more details about Addie.

"We were very close, Addie and I," Selah Ann began. "Marvin and I used to live with Addie and her husband, Henry Marsh, in Richmond, Virginia, when we were first married. Addie talked a great deal to me about her baby she had given up for adoption, always with tears in her eyes. When she visited her family in Goldsboro, she told me that she made a point of walking past the Weil house and then to Herman Park at the end of the street to try to get a glimpse of you playing with your cousin, Ruthie. She seemed to know when you were visiting the Weils."

"It must have been very painful for her and I imagine she had suffered greatly when she gave me up for adoption. Oh, how I wish I could have known her." Then, thoughtfully, I asked, "Do you know why she named me Julia?"

"You were named for your Aunt Julia, Addie's favorite aunt, who could not bear children. She and her husband, Lawrence Edward Newsom, wanted to adopt you, but thought better of it because of their close relationship to Addie. Instead, they adopted another baby daughter and named her Mary Helen. Many people thought that Mary Helen was really Addie's baby, until you surfaced, of course. The Newsoms live in Lucama around the corner from me. Mary Helen married Daryl Simpson and they also live in Lucama."

My birth mother, Addie Pate Marsh, wearing bobby socks and saddle shoes, (age 36), one year before her death. Norfolk, VA, 1941.

At Kingswood School Cranbrook, wearing bobby socks and saddle shoes, (age 17), one year before my graduation. Bloomfield Hills, MI. 1941.

My appetite for information was insatiable, so I asked another question. "Why was I given the middle name of Rowena?" "I really don't know," Selah Ann answered. "Perhaps Addie was reading Sir Walter Scott's novel, Ivanhoe, and admired the character, Lady Rowena, queen of love and beauty." This seemed a romantic solution to my name, and I relished the idea.

"I have a photograph for you," Selah Ann said. "Addie knew that I was acquainted with the Weil family and hoped someday I might meet you." As she handed me the photograph, she added, "Addie wanted you to have this. It was taken in 1941, the year before she died."

I stared at the picture of my birth mother, who was sitting on a stone wall wearing a skirt, sweater, bobby socks and saddle shoes, much like I had worn in 1941. She looked so young and happy. I was thrilled, once more, at recognizing our resemblance to each other.

Selah Ann told me Addie was hit by a car while crossing the street in Richmond in the fall of 1942. Had she not been wearing a fur coat, she would have been killed. The coat helped to soften the blow. While recovering in the hospital, she developed a kidney infection and died on December 23, 1942. She was only thirty-seven years old. This was the year in which I graduated from Kingswood School Cranbrook, when I was eighteen years old. (Addie was nineteen years old when she gave birth to me.) December 23 was the same day I received my first photograph of Addie in 1983, and also the same day as Tom's funeral in 1984; a chilling coincidence!

I learned a great deal from Selah Ann, and I was grateful to her for providing me with more information about Addie.

It was time to return to Smithfield as we were going to another Pate get-together that evening in Goldsboro.

Jack, Judy, their children and Lillie Mae were invited this time, along with some of the Pates and Sassers who had never met. I was happy to be the one to bring them together at this gathering for the first time. The only ones missing were my two sisters, Waudelle and Lauretta, and I vowed that at the next Pate reunion, we all would be there together.

Driving back to Smithfield, I reflected upon my visit with Jack and his family. I had become fast friends with Lillie Mae, respecting and admiring her, and I felt very close to Jack and Judy. Arriving at their house, an unexpected pleasure lay before me.

"How would you like to sleep in a water bed?" Jack asked. "You may have your choice of Jay's water bed or Jacque's conventional bed."

Of course, I chose the water bed, thinking it might be my only opportunity for such an experience. As I climbed in, I questioned how two people would keep their equilibrium and manage the wake of the water simultaneously. It provided me with a "floating over the waves" sensation. To my surprise, I slept soundly and reported no aches or pains in the morning.

143

Chapter Thirty-four
A Coup de Foudre!

*T*he summer of '85 was filled with plans to spend the month of July with my children and grandchildren at our cottage on Northport Point, Michigan, along the shores of Grand Traverse Bay. I looked forward to the cool breezes, the fresh smell of pine and the welcoming screeches of the seagulls.

My daughter, Meg, and her husband, Robert Marshall Carlson, had just been divorced. My son, Tom, and his wife, Leslie Matthews, had been divorced a few years before. It was unfortunate that they were not with us, because I love Bob and Leslie and still consider them part of our family.

That summer, Meg met Warner Arms Peck III, whose family owns a cottage on the Point. "Army" had been divorced for several years and has two children. Their romance blossomed during the summer and plans were made for a fall wedding.

An acquaintance of mine, Bill Wotherspoon, is another cottage owner on the Point. Bill lost his wife, Mary Bulkley

(Buckle), to cancer just two months after Tom's death. Although I did not know Bill well, I thought it might be nice to re-acquaint myself, since we had a loss in common. One day, when I was grocery shopping at the local market, my cart accidentally bumped into Bill's cart, as I hurriedly rounded a corner. For me it was a "coup de foudre!" Was he aware of it? I wondered later.

"I'm so sorry," I stammered. "How nice to see you, Bill. I've been thinking about you and wondering how you are getting along," I added nervously. He was handsome, tall, trim, sun-tanned, and had graying hair. His brown eyes were so dark that his pupils were barely visible. As we stood talking, I decided I wouldn't let him pass through the narrow aisle until we made a commitment to get together. Since women usually take the initiative, I boldly asked, "How would you like to come to our cottage for a drink this evening? My daughter, Mimi, and her family are here, and we are planning to go to Woody's Settling Inn for dinner. It would be fun if you would join us. Is there anyone with you in your cottage? If so, bring them along."

"No, I'm alone and I'm waiting to pick up some fish I ordered for my dinner tonight."

"Freeze it," I said with a smile. He hesitated, then shyly suggested, "Uh, why don't you come to my house for a drink instead? I'll show you my garden." "You mean all of us?" I questioned.

"No, I mean just you," he answered, and grinned sheepishly, making my heart skip a beat.

"Then, will you join us for dinner?" I asked. It was a wonderful evening and I thoroughly enjoyed his company. I wanted to see more of him but, unfortunately, I was leaving for Toledo the next day. I had made previous plans to fly to Montana with the Barnums to visit the Baileys, stopping first in Oshkosh, Wisconsin, to see the National Air Show. I asked my daughters to keep an eye on Bill until I returned three weeks later. Meg reported, when I telephoned later in the summer, "I've seen him on the golf course, Mom, and he has great legs."

Chapter Thirty-five
Flying to Montana

*M*y trip with the Barnums was full of adventure. At Oshkosh, the three of us slept in sleeping bags under one of the wings of Tony's amphibious plane, which was tethered to the ground, wing to wing, next to hundreds of other kinds of aircraft. Constantly, airplanes buzzed overhead; colorful parachutists floated down to earth; the Blue Angels performed with daring precision and the new French Concord maneuvered at a low altitude and frightful speed. Old World War II planes and new air-propelled inventions were on display. It was a fascinating sight. Because of his love for flying, I couldn't help but think how much Tom would have enjoyed this trip. I missed him desperately.

Flying on to Montana was just as eventful. We flew over forested mountains, checkered board farm fields and miles of uncultivated land. We could see herds of antelope bounding over the plains below us. Tony maneuvered his plane through canyons and valleys with huge trees looming up on either side. Suddenly we broke out into the open over Swan Lake, where the Baileys were waiting. After indicating our arrival by buzzing the cabin and waving our wings, Tony skimmed over the lake to look for dangerous rocks or obstacles to be avoided before making his landing approach. Then, he neatly settled down on the water directly in front of the Bailey's log cabin.

What a spectacular spot they developed. A tennis court and garden surrounded their handsome cabin. Big Fork was the closest town, a charming village with live theater and western art galleries. Bob Terhune, a friend from Northport Point, suggested I contact his artist friend, Hank Lawshè. He was not difficult to find, as he was exhibiting his Western paintings in one of the galleries.

"Would you like to come out to Swan Lake?" I asked him. "The view of the mountains mirrored on the lake is spectacular. We could paint together." And so we did. Our oil painting now hangs on the living room wall of the Bailey's cabin.

As always, it was a "circus" being with the Barnums and Baileys, my good friends, who made this a special trip to help lift my spirits.

Chapter Thirty-six
Getting to Know Bill

*W*ith great anticipation of seeing Bill, I drove back to Northport Point for the remainder of the summer. On our first date, we dined at the Blue Bird Inn in Leland, twelve miles from Northport.

"I have so much to tell you, Bill," I said, and I poured forth my story about finding my roots. I wanted him to know all about me. I could not stop my flow of words. What have I done? I prattled on like a magpie, and he must have been bored to death. Catching myself from monopolizing the conversation, I questioned him about his life.

"Well, I am a fifth generation Washingtonian, and graduated from Dartmouth College. I became a commissioned officer in the Navy before the war," he began. "In 1941 I was sent to Detroit as a Naval Ordnance Inspector. While visiting in Grosse Pointe, I met Buckle. After the war began, I left Detroit and went to the Naval War College in Newport, Rhode Island, then to Africa and Europe. I worked at different times with Douglas Fairbanks, Jr. and Harold

McMillan, but never lost interest in my girl from Grosse Pointe. After the war ended, I returned to Grosse Pointe and married Buckle in 1946. Then, I went to work for the Ford Motor Company." He continued to tell me, "One of my interests is gardening. I raise orchids in my greenhouse in Grosse Pointe."

He was a man of many talents, and at the end of the evening, I found myself enjoying his company immensely and looked forward to seeing him again. Indeed, for the remaining weeks in August, we did see a great deal of each other. We played golf, tennis, and talked about our common interests in art, music and skiing. As the summer came to an end, Bill said, "I'm planning a ski trip to Lech, Austria, next winter. Would you like to go with me?"

"Go with you, alone!?!" I was shocked and swallowed hard. My first thought was that I should ask permission. But from whom? My children? My dog? I was aware that people of the opposite sex often traveled together and gave it no thought, but I was from the old school. Bill must have read my mind, because he added, "I think my daughters, Polly and Ellie, are planning to go. You could ask your son, Tom, to join us." That sounded like a good idea to me.

"Meg and Army are getting married on October 5th in Toledo and there will be a lot to do before then. But, after the wedding, I'll have plenty of time to make plans for a skiing trip. I've never skied in Europe and it sounds wonderful," I said almost breathlessly. "All right, knowing how busy you'll be, I'll wait until after the wedding to call you," he promised.

Their marriage took place at home in our living room in front of the fireplace. The mantle was banked with white roses, ivy and candles. The Reverend Robert Wuellner from the First Congregational Church performed the ceremony. It was a small wedding, including Meg's two sons, Todd and Scott; Army's two children, Warner IV and Patty; and other close family members. Afterward, a dinner dance was held at the Belmont Country Club. The happy couple planned to live in Indianapolis, Indiana, where Army was a vice-president of the Huber, Hunt and Nichol Construction Company.

Chapter Thirty-seven
Will You Marry Me?

*M*onday morning after the wedding, just as I was wondering if Bill really would remember to call me, the telephone rang. His voice sounded alive and refreshing. I told him about a special exhibit at the Toledo Museum of Art of Spanish still life paintings. "It is exquisite. Would you like to see it?" I asked. "Of course," he answered.

He arrived on my doorstep the next day holding a sprig of rosemary he had picked from his garden. It was lovely and brought to mind a poem my mother often quoted.

> "There's a word in language spoken,
> That holds a memory dear.
> In English, 'tis for-get-me-not.
> In French, 'tis souvenir."

That was the beginning of his many drives to Toledo from his home in Grosse Pointe Farms, Michigan. While he was in Toledo, I introduced him to my friends. He invited me to join him in Detroit for theater and opera and to Grosse Pointe for parties to meet his friends.

In late October, we went to Northport Point, where we find autumn breathtakingly beautiful. The trees are at the height of their color change, and the harvest moon shimmers serenely on the lake. It was in this romantic setting, sitting close to each other by a roaring fire, that Bill asked me to marry him.

We picked December 28, 1985 for our wedding date, so each of us could spend Christmas with our respective families. Therefore, many plans had to be finalized before Christmas. As Thanksgiving was approaching, Bill asked me to spend the holiday in Washington, D.C. He wanted me to meet his family: his one sister, "Skiddy," and her husband, Captain A. Elmore "Sonny" Miller, Jr., and their children. Polly and Ellie joined us. Bill met my cousins-in-law, the Haleys and Flues, who knew the Millers. We were one big, happy family. At a later date, we visited Bill's other sister, Anne, and her husband, W. Ogden Ross, in Newport, Rhode Island.

Most of our children and friends had made previous plans to leave Toledo and Grosse Pointe the day after Christmas. Our wedding was to be just the two of us with Reverend Robert Wuellner officiating in the chapel of the First Congregational Church in Toledo. When it became known that no one was invited to attend the ceremony, my friends, the Barnums and Urschels, announced, "You can't get married without us. It wouldn't be legal. We're coming to share in your happiness."

Tommy, Mickey and Steve, and my grandchildren, John and Maggie, were my only family members left in Toledo. "Mom, we have to come to your wedding in order to support the family," Steve said. "Besides, I have a video camera, and I want to record it." Of course, we could not refuse and were happy to have them all there.

My marriage to William Wallace Wotherspoon.
December 28, 1985.

Bill and I drove to Northport Point to spend our first honeymoon. Two weeks later, we flew to Austria for our second honeymoon. Polly and Ellie joined us at Lech, but Tommy declined our invitation as he was busy with his new duties as President and Chairman of the Board of Spartan Chemical Co. The weather was very cold, and there was so much snow and wind it was difficult to ski. The ambiance and charm, however, of the the Walch Family Lodge, "Angela," and the little village of Lech nestled in the Austrian Arlberg, made up for the inclement weather.

At the lodge, perched halfway up the mountain, German was the spoken language. Place cards were used every night at dinner and ours read, "Herr and Frau Wasser-Löffel," (water-spoon). This seemed to be their closest German translation for Wotherspoon. I began calling Bill, Wasser, then Wassi and Was. Hence, his nickname, Wassi! (pronounced "V"assi) My children call me "Mama-Rooh" (Mary Ruth), therefore Bill became "Wassa-Rooh."

Chapter Thirty-eight
Mutual Adjustments

$\mathcal{I}$t was not until April, 1986, that I moved permanently into Wassi's house in Grosse Pointe Farms. Many adjustments for both of us had to be made. I needed to sort out my belongings and sell my house in Toledo. Then one day Mimi said to me, "Mark and I would like to buy your house, Mom."

Farewell to Duke, my Belgian Sheepdog. March, 1986.

I could not have been happier than to have my daughter and her husband live in the house that Tom and I had built and in which she had been raised. To have it kept in the family delighted me.

The only unsolved problem was what to do with my Belgian sheep dog, Duke. Wassi could not have him because of his pool and beautiful garden. Mimi could not keep him because her dog, Ty, and Duke did not get along. I had to give Duke away. It was one of the hardest tasks I had ever had to perform. He was my faithful companion, my comfort during the past year, and I loved him dearly. I found a

new home for him in the country with horses and other Belgian sheep dogs. I think of him often, and wonder if he misses me as much as I miss him.

Wassi and I had so many interests in common it was easy to make plans for our future. When we were in Grosse Pointe, there were symphonies, operas, theater and art exhib-

With Wassi in Arizona, 1988.

its that we shared. When we traveled, there were ski trips in Michigan and Colorado, vacations in Arizona, trips with the Archives of American Art to Europe, and a North Cape cruise. One spring, our garden was open to the members of the Garden Club of America. The next year, I became a member of the Garden Club of Michigan, the Scarab Club and the Grosse Pointe Artists Association. I resumed painting and began exhibiting my work. Wassi started playing the guitar again, and I continued with my aerobic dancing and conversational French with L'Alliance Française de Grosse Pointe. Aside from our separate activities, we ice skated, golfed, played tennis, and took ballroom dancing lessons together. Our lives were full.

Skiing with Wassi in Colorado.
February / March, 1987.

Chapter Thirty-nine
Wassi Meets My "Kinfolk"

*I*n June of 1988, three years after we were married, there was another Pate reunion in Goldsboro. Wassi was eager to meet my newfound family after hearing so much about my successful search. We flew with Tommy in the Spartan plane, once again, to North Carolina.

With Tommy and Wassi at the Second Pate Reunion, June, 1987.

Joyce and Paul met us at the airport and drove us to St. Luke United Methodist Church where Waudelle, Lauretta and their husbands greeted us. "I am so happy to see you again, and all of the other Pate families," I said. Selah Ann and her son, Marvin Pate Jr., were there. I had not met Marvin before and his resemblance to Tommy was astounding. Their profiles were identical, with their high foreheads and pug noses. My grandson, T. J., follows suit.

After introducing Wassi to my "kinfolk," we all sat down this time to a delicious Southern fried chicken dinner. Following dinner, Albert Pate stood up and gave an interesting disseration on the first Pates, namely

Marvin Pate, Jr. and Tommy (identical profiles). June, 1988.

Thoroughgood Pate, who settled in Roquis Pocosin (Turtle Swamp), which later became Wayne County, North Carolina, in the early 1700s. "The Pate clan lived up to their Welsh heritage," he declared. "These Pates were tough and prolific and their conflicts with the Indians were numerous and bloody. The settlement of Patetown evolved due to the many Pates living in this area outside of Goldsboro." Years later I was to learn that my biological parents, Addie Pate and Jake Sasser, lived and were buried in Patetown.

Before we left Toledo, I had notified Jack that we would be attending another Pate reunion, but would be in Goldsboro for only one day.

"Would it be possible for us to see you in the afternoon, just before we fly back home?" I asked. "I want Wassi to meet you."

"Wonderful," Jack replied. "We're all anxious to meet Bill. Can you be at Mother's house about 3 p.m.?"

Our visit was short, but it was marvelous to see Jack, Judy, Lillie Mae and some of the Sasser family again.

"Jack, I feel guilty that you and my sisters are here in the Goldsboro area this very minute, yet have never met. I'm sorry this could not have been arranged ahead of time. At the next Pate reunion, my Sasser family will be included. I will see to it. I promise!"

Part Six

So Here We Are

Chapter Forty
Travels with Wassi

For the next few years, Wassi and I continued with our wide range of activities. One very special occasion was Wassi's seventieth birthday on September 24, 1989. We celebrated by giving a dinner dance at The Grosse Pointe Club, to which all of our combined families and friends were invited. It was the first time we had been able to gather all of our children together for a family photograph. Although our summers at Northport Point included spending time with our families, seldom was everyone there at the same time.

Another special occasion was Wassi's fiftieth class reunion at Dartmouth College in Hanover, New Hampshire in June 1990.

"I really have no desire to go back to Dartmouth," he told me. "I won't know a soul, and no one will know me."

"But, I've never been to Dartmouth," I urged, "and I would love to see the campus." So we went! It turned out, as I suspected. He recognized more friends, and they him, than he had ever imagined. We

Wassi's 70th Birthday

Back row: Steve and Mickey Swigart, Ellie Wotherspoon, Army Peck, Polly Wotherspoon, Mark Smith, Tom Swigart. Front Row: Meg Peck, Mary Ruth and Bill Wotherspoon, Mimi Smith. The Grosse Pointe Club, Grosse Pointe Farms, Michigan, September 24, 1992.

even came upon an old photograph of him with his rowing team still hanging on the boathouse wall. From Hanover we drove to Stowe, Vermont, where we stayed at the Von Trapp Family Lodge. The beautiful mountains and quaint East Coast villages were a refreshing relief from the hubbub of the fast-moving life in Detroit.

Having often skied in Colorado, the next winter we decided to try Deer Valley, Utah. We stayed at the Stein Eriksen Lodge. Stein, Olympic gold medalist and world-champion skier, had taught the Swigart family to ski at Boyne Mountain, Michigan, in the mid-fifties. I was anxious to see him again. He hadn't changed, was as handsome as ever, and still skied like a graceful bird in flight. One day I said to him, "Stein, with these well-groomed slopes, this is a perfect ski resort for the old folks." He grinned, put his arm around me and replied in his charming Norwegian accent, "'V'e're never too old to ski, Mary."

Our friends, the Barnums and Baileys, joined us for a few days, making it a fun reunion as they also had skied with Stein at Boyne Mountain.

In order to warm our bones from the chilling Utah winds, we planned a Southern trip in the Spring to Hopetown, Abaco in the Bahama Islands. The quaint, once British-owned colony, with its pastel painted cottages, red and white candy-striped lighthouse befriending the entrance to the tiny harbor and soft warm breezes, was a welcome change. It was there we arranged a short visit with our English friends, Polly and David Grose.

Tommy, who was on the Spartan boat in Fort Lauderdale vacationing with his son, T. J., contacted us and asked, "Mom, how would you like me to fly to Hopetown, pick you up in the Spartan plane and fly you back to Florida to spend a couple of days with us on the Hidilution?" Before we knew it, he was buzzing the

With Stein Eriksen.
Deer Valley, Utah,
1991.

Peggy and Paul Bailey.
Deer Valley, Utah, 1991.

Jeane and Tony Barnum.
Northport Point, Michi-
gan, August, 1991.

Abaco Inn and arriving by ferry boat from Marsh Harbor, where he had landed the plane.

With our bare feet in the sand, we greeted them. After a swim and lunch, we flew back to Florida and spent the next few days sailing in the ocean and up and down the intercoastal waterway. The contrast between island life and city life was dramatic.

The following fall, we were invited to Wassi's niece's wedding in St. Croix in the U.S. Virgin Islands. We accepted with pleasure, anxious to put our feet back into the warm sand again. Not only did we accomplish this, but we were informed by the bride: "The wedding will take place on a catamaran and everyone is required to be barefooted. 'Big Beard', the captain, who is also a minister, will perform the ceremony at sea."

The bride in white lace, the groom in tuxedo, the captain and twenty-some guests in assorted garb of slacks, shorts, and dresses, all abided by the rules—no shoes! It was an unusual and charming wedding, not to be forgotten.

172

Chapter Forty-one
The Elkhorn Ranch

$\mathcal{I}$t was always my desire to take my children and grandchildren on a family vacation. My mother had taken our family, all six of us, on our memorable Mediterranean cruise in 1961, and thirty years later, I wanted to repeat a similar trip. The problem was, there were eighteen of us now. We could not decide where to go and never were able to go at the same time. Suddenly it seemed to fall into place when Wassi suggested, "Why don't you take them to The Elkhorn Ranch, south of Tucson, Arizona, over Thanksgiving?" "That's a perfect solution," I said, "but plans must be arranged immediately."

Wassi and I had been there before and loved the riding and the casual living in the West. We had also vacationed at The Elkhorn Ranch in Montana during the summer of 1990. That same summer we visited with the Baileys on Swan Lake, drove through Glacier National Park, and then stopped at Big Sky Ski Resort before arriving at Elkhorn. Wassi's daughter, Ellie, met us at the Ranch. During our stay, I met a young woman connected with independent film documentaries, who listened to my tale about the search for my identity. While talking with her, I recalled many of my friends having said to me, "Oh Mary, you should write a book. This is such a wonderful story." But after Tom's long illness and subsequent death, and then my marriage to Wassi, I found myself too busy and I had lost the enthusiasm for such a project. With the retelling of my search, my interest was rekindled.

"What do you think about my writing a book?" I questioned her. "Perhaps my story would make an interesting film documentary. Since my half-sisters have never met my half-brother, I plan to bring them together for the first time." She encouraged the idea of my being the common denominator of their first union. Such a meeting, she suggested, would create a happy conclusion to my story.

Keeping her suggestion in mind as my goal, I flung myself into the writing of this book in the fall of 1990, along with planning our family Thanksgiving gathering for the following year.

The Elkhorn Ranch in Arizona, like the Elkhorn Ranch in Montana, was well run by the members of the Miller family. There were plenty of horses for all. We hoped that Wassi's daughters, Polly and Ellie, would join us at the ranch over Thanksgiving, but they were unable to do so. As the time drew nearer, I was afraid someone in my family might have to cancel at the last minute.

They all planned to arrive late the night before Thanksgiving. I hardly slept—straining my ears for the sounds of approaching cars which I never heard. Early the next morning, Wassi went outside to investigate and came running back with tears in his eyes.

"They're all here!" he exclaimed.

Immediately, I began to cry, as I was overwhelmed with joy. "We made it, Mom, all eighteen of us," they shouted excitedly.

My grandchildren ranged in ages from six to sixteen. Together we all rode up the steep rocky trails into the mountains. They swam, and played tennis, shuffle board and ping pong. The boys enjoyed the pistol/rifle range and Steve, with his son, John (both avid golfers), found a nearby course. At night, we played charades and a wrangler sang Western songs to the strumming of his guitar. On the last night, there was a square dance in which all participated, young and old. Meg gave us matching cowgirl and cowboy tee-shirts to wear for our family photograph.

It was a very wonderful Thanksgiving and, best of all, no one had to cook a turkey!

Family gathering at The Elkhorn Ranch, Tucson, Arizona. Thanksgiving, 1991.

Chapter Forty-two
A Retrospective Art Exhibit

𝒯or the first time in my life, I was not with my family at Christmas, but since we had all been together over Thanksgiving,

Self-portrait, pastel, 20 x 26. 1992.

we decided to spend the holiday at Northport Point with Polly and Ellie. Many of the cottage owners were there, so the Point was jumping with bright lights and parties. A few days of skiing at nearby Sugar Loaf Ski Resort helped us get into shape for our second ski trip to Deer Valley, Utah, in early February, 1992. We flew home from Utah in time to attend Wassi's Aunt "Boofie's" (Ruth Larner

Oliphant) 100th birthday celebration on February 26th at the Metropolitan Club in Washington, D.C. She was alert and spry—a remarkable woman!

During the next few months I was busy getting ready for my "one person" art exhibition, which was scheduled for the month of May at the Scarab Club in Detroit. In March, I completed a pastel self-portrait to be exhibited in the show.

Napa Valley,
California.
April, 1992.

In April, we took a trip to Napa Valley, California. Several months before, we had attended a benefit dinner and wine auction for The Center for Creative Studies, which was held at The Edsel and Eleanor Ford House, and we "won" the seven day Napa Valley trip. This consisted of visits to many wineries and vineyards nestled in the beautiful valley. The highlight of our trip was a private dinner with Blanche and Peter Mondavi in their lovely home built next to the winery, and a private lunch with Elizabeth and Louis Martini in their charming home; an old converted winery. To taste their wines and be given personal tours of their wineries and vineyards was a special treat. We learned a great deal from our two charming hosts who, with their fathers, were winemaking pioneers in the Valley.

We spent two days in San Francisco with Katherine

178

Sanger Dalgero, my only cousin on the Sanger side of the family. I told Kay about the search for my identity. Having just lost her husband and without children, I think it was difficult for her to grasp my feelings about wanting to search for my roots. It is sad to think that she is the last of the Sanger line.

Saturday, May 2nd was the opening reception of my art exhibition in Detroit. It began with a charcoal self-

With Waudelle, Lauretta and Shirley. Scarab Club Exhibition Reception. Detroit, Michigan, May 2, 1992.

portrait I had drawn at the age of fifteen in 1939, and ended with my recent pastel self-portrait (1992). This retrospective collection of sixty-six paintings, prints and drawings was displayed in the lounge gallery of the Scarab Club, an historical building nestled in the Cultural Center of the city behind the Detroit Institute of Arts.

My first "one person" art exhibition was in 1967 in Toledo. It was held in the newly-expanded Sigmond Sanger Branch Library. The library is named for my father, who had been president of the Board of Directors of The Toledo Public Library for thirty years before his death. I felt honored to be the first exhibitor.

Much has transpired in my life between these two art exhibitions, but finding my roots is the project which has completely engulfed my thoughts and consumed my energy. I keep in touch with my half-siblings, Waudelle, Lauretta and Jack, especially over the holiday seasons and their birthdays, often reminding them of our upcoming Pate reunion in Goldsboro in August 1992, where they will meet for the first time.

A few days before the opening of my Scarab Club exhibition, the telephone rang. "We wanted to surprise you, but thought better of it. Lauretta, our cousin, Shirley Warren, and I are coming to Detroit for the opening." Waudelle announced. "We have made all of our arrangements and we're very anxious to see you and your work."

I was stunned! "You mean you are coming all the way from Texas, Lauretta from Virginia and Shirley from North Carolina just to see my show?" I couldn't believe it. "That is fantastic!" I continued, "I can't wait to see you all." I was elated to think that my sisters and first cousin would make such an effort. To be part of such a caring family made me feel honored and proud.

The opening was a huge success. Nearly one hundred guests attended the reception. My family, friends and relatives came from Toledo, as well as many friends from Grosse Pointe. A beautiful bouquet of flowers arrived from my friends "Les Femmes" in Toledo and another from Erma Zerner. Two lovely baskets of flowers were given to me from Betsy Campbell and Ellen Thurber, friends in Grosse Pointe. Photographs were taken, and Steve recorded the event with his trusty video camera. I was happy Waudelle, Lauretta and Shirley were able to see my family again and meet my friends.

At breakfast the next morning, I asked my sisters and Shirley, "What about the reunion plans?"

"We are planning a pig-pickin' at Clara Pate Garris' house on Saturday, August 1st," Shirley answered. "Audrey Garris Smith and I are working on the arrangements."

"That sounds wonderful! Don't forget to invite my brother Jack and his family. I would like Lillie Mae to be included too." I was not sure how she would feel about Jack meeting my sisters, but I hoped she would be receptive to the occasion. I did not want to hurt her. "I am very anxious to have you all meet," I added.

Saying goodbye to them didn't seem so hard, as I knew that I would be seeing them again in a few months.

Chapter Forty-three
At Last, My Half-Sisters and Half-Brother Meet!

$\mathcal{E}$arly in June, 1992, I attended my 50th class reunion at Kingswood School Cranbrook. What fun it was to become re-acquainted with so many of my classmates. We reminisced and exchanged family photographs. "Of course, 'no one has changed'," we all declared. I couldn't wait to tell them about my search, and the book I was writing. Wassi and I spent July and August at his cottage at Northport Point, and my children and grandchildren shared the Swigart cottage nearby. It was always fun to get together and enjoy the usual summer activities of golf, tennis, swimming and boating with our families. The Pate reunion was sandwiched between these two months, on August 1st.

As the date drew nearer, I was told there had been a change in the Pate reunion plans. Clara Pate Garris' daughter, Geraldine Cuneo, who lived in New York, was gravely ill. Therefore, instead of having a pig-pickin'

at Clara's house, we were to have the reunion at The Stoney Creek Free Will Baptist Church in Patetown. A new addition to the church had been built, which included a large air-conditioned reception hall for which we were all thankful, since temperatures soared in the Carolinas at that time of the year. A few days before we were to leave for North Carolina, Tommy and his sixteen year old son, T. J., flew from Toledo to Northport in the Spartan airplane. The pilot, Jim Lenardson, his wife Penny, and Tommy's friend Dawn Kemp were with him. T. J. planned to stay with his cousins at the Swigart cottage while we were at the reunion.

Finally, the long anticipated day arrived. It was early on Saturday morning, August 1, 1992, when Wassi and I drove to the Traverse City airport with Tommy and the others to board The Spartan King-Air in which, once again, we were to make our flight to Goldsboro, North Carolina. Jim and Tommy flew pilot and co-pilot respectively. Penny was to be our official photographer. It was an easy two and-one half hour flight. Our two rental cars took us from the Goldsboro airport to the church in Patetown in time for lunch.

As we opened the large double doors to the church's new hall, we were delighted to see nearly one hundred members of the Pate family gathered inside. My eyes scanned the room in search of Jack, Waudelle and Lauretta. I couldn't wait to see them. I tingled with anticipation at the thought of their first meeting.

Everyone greeted us eagerly. It was wonderful to see so many of them again, but there had been sad changes in some of their lives. Joyce had lost her husband, Paul. Eva had had a stroke and was wheelchair bound. Jack's mother, Lillie Mae, was unable to join us because she, too, had suffered a series of small strokes.

Jack, Judy, their son Jay, and his family were there with Jack and Judy's first grandson, Jacob. Waudelle and Ben had their daughter Debbie and her husband Mark with them. Lauretta and Bill were alone.

When I was finally able to gather my siblings together for introductions, I hardly knew what was being said. All I could do was to look with wonderment at the three of them. The other faces in the room became a blur. When I recovered my composure, I found Penny

Judy Sasser's reaction to my siblings' first meeting. Patetown, North Carolina. August 1, 1992.

was snapping her camera. She had captured the long awaited moment on film. The ecstatic look on Judy's face expressed the total joy of that first meeting between my Pate and Sasser siblings.

After forming a line for the delicious buffet luncheon, we found places to sit at long tables and chatted with my "kinfolk." Everyone brought assorted platters of Southern fried chicken, country ham, barbecued pork, casseroles, salads, breads, biscuits, baked beans and homemade cakes and pies. Our contribution was six quarts of large sweet black cherries grown near our cottage in the Leelanau County Peninsula. This is one of the largest areas of cherry orchards in the world.

Following much picture taking and the scrumptious lunch, Audrey Garris Smith presided over the gathering. One person from each family group spoke. Some showed photographs, others told of their recent marriages, births and deaths.

Clara Pate Garris, struggling to stand up from her chair, said in a quavering voice, "I want to make sure that the old people are not forgotten. I think that I'm the oldest one here." (She is in her late eighties, close to the age Addie would have been.) When it was my turn to speak, I introduced my family and friends who came with me, then added that after the search for my identity, it had been my long-held dream to bring my three siblings together for the first time. "Today at this reunion it is accomplished," I proudly announced. I also told them how pleased I was that Waudelle, Lauretta and Shirley Warren had traveled so far from their respective homes in Texas, Virginia and North Carolina for the opening of my art exhibition in Detroit last May. I passed around a photograph album of my paintings.

After the meeting, Jack was eager to have us visit Lillie Mae.

"Do you think your mother really wants to meet Waudelle and Lauretta?" I asked, recalling her initial reluctance to acknowledge me or tell Jack about me in 1984.

"Oh, yes," he said, "Mother is anxious to see all of us. But we'd better hurry as she has been waiting and tires easily."

We crossed the road to Lillie Mae's house. She looked frail, but very pretty, dressed in a pink silk négligé and sitting upright in a chair. She held a tiny rubber football in her right hand. Determined to improve after her strokes, she squeezed it to strengthen her hand and arm.

"I am so happy to see you again, Lillie Mae," I said as I kissed her. "I would like you to meet my half-sisters, Waudelle Strickley from Texas and Lauretta Dixon from Virginia. They are Addie's daughters, too."

She seemed delighted to meet them and spoke fondly of Addie, once more revealing Addie's many meetings with Jake at her house on Sunday afternoons after church. Before we left, she asked Jack to show my sisters some photographs of Jake. When we said goodbye, I had a sad premonition that this would be the last time I would see her.

We were staying at the same Holiday Inn in Goldsboro where my sisters and I first met in 1984. After checking in and refreshing ourselves, we gathered for dinner at The River Haus Restaurant—all twenty-two of us. Joyce, Shirley, Cora Lee and Charles Beamon joined us. How wonderful it was to be together. Cameras flashed everywhere. Jack and Judy bade us goodbye soon after dinner. They were momentarily expecting the birth of identical twin grandsons. "We are thrilled for you," I said. "Be sure to let us know when the big event occurs. Kiss the new babies for us and bring them to the next reunion."

The following morning we said our goodbyes to Waudelle and Lauretta over breakfast. I told them how much we would be looking forward to our next re-union.

As we were preparing to board the King-Air to fly back to Northern Michigan, Mary Helen and Daryl Simpson surprised us by coming to the airport to see us off. They filled our arms with delicious red tomatoes and green peppers, freshly picked from their garden. As we climbed aboard, I heard Mary Helen say to Daryl, "Gotta' go! They're gettin' ready to hit the air." We chuckled and blew them a kiss.

While circling over Patetown, I reflected upon the

many memories I will cherish of this special Pate reunion that brought my siblings and me together at last. I was the common denominator of this meeting, and the reunion was a successful culmination of my ten year search for my identity. I experienced feelings of tremendous relief, satisfaction and accomplishment.

Wassi, Mary Ruth, Mary Helen and Daryl Simpson at Goldsboro, North Carolina Airport, August, 1992.

The life-long burden of wondering "where did I come from?" has been lifted from my shoulders. I am blessed to have discovered I belong to two additional families, the Pates and the Sassers, who have enriched my life. While distances keep us apart more than we would like, loving thoughts bind us together. We are always just a greeting card or a telephone call away.

I have found my identity, my two half-sisters and my half-brother. Now I am proud and elated to say,

"So here we are!"

SO HERE WE ARE!
Waudelle, Mary Ruth, Jack, Lauretta.
Patetown, North Carolina, August 1, 1992.

Appendix

I. PERSONS

Boggs, Dr. L. W.,
   Hospital Medical Records of,
   Greenville, South Carolina, 38, 72

Carrére, Charlotte, geneologist,
Goldsboro, North Carolina,
68-69, 71,75,79,80,101,103,108

Ludeman, Judge, 51-52

Marsh, Addie Ernestine Pate
   marriage record of, 79
   death record of, 79

Pate, Addie Ernestine (birth mother)
   birth record, 79

Pinkerton Investigators, 51-2,55,60 (See Agencies
under Sources)

Sasser, Jacob Calvin (Jake) (biological father)
   birth record of, 108
   marriage record of, 108
   death record of, 108

Smolowe, Greta, psychic,
Rabbit Skin Road,
Asheville, North Carolina, 73-4

II. PLACES

Children's Home Society of North Carolina,
Goldsboro, North Carolina, 55

Churches
Jesus Christ of Latter Day Saints, Church of,
1545 Eastgate, Toledo, Ohio, 69

Mormon Tabernacle,
50 E. Temple,
Salt Lake City, Utah 84150
(801) 240-1000,
69 (Complete U.S. Census Records)

Court House Records, Wayne County,
North Carolina, 55

County Clerk of Court Birth Ledger,
Greenville, South Carolina, 77

County Court House Record Book, old,
Greenville, South Carolina, 73, 76-7

Deans Cemetery,
Goldsboro, North Carolina, 67, 79, 121

Editor, News Argus,
Goldsboro, North Carolina, 67

Health and Environmental Control, Department of,
2600 Bull Street,
Columbia, South Carolina 29201,
51, 73, 76

Health and Environmental Control, Department of,
200 University Ridge,
Greenville, South Carolina 29601,
51, 72, 76-7

Historical Society Room, Wayne County,
Goldsboro, North Carolina, 67

Libraries
Fort Wayne Allen County Public Library,
900 Webster Street,
Fort Wayne, Indiana 46862,
69

Census and Geneology, Department of, 69

Goldsboro Public Library,
Goldsboro, North Carolina, 67

Jesus Christ of Latter Day Saints, Church of,
Geneology Library, Department of, 69
records from Mormon Tabernacle Church, Salt Lake City,
Utah) See Churches

Sanger Library, Branch,
2753 W. Central Avenue, Toledo, Ohio 43606
(419) 259-5370,
179

Toledo Lucas County Public Library,
6749 Monroe Street, Toledo, Ohio 43560,
69

Lucas County Children's Home,
Toledo, Ohio 43614
records from, 69, 75-6
ward of, 53, 80

Lucas County Probate Court, Toledo Ohio
adoption papers, copies of, 51-3
records from, 69

Mortuary
Seymour Funeral Home,
1300 Wayne Memorial Drive,
Goldsboro, North Carolina, 67

Sources

I. **AGENCIES**
Pinkerton Security and Investigation Services,
Consult Detective Agencies in Yellow Pages
Telephone Directory.

II. **ARTICLES**
Adopted Have The Same Rights As Others (The),
Marlene Piasecki. New York Times, October 30,
1990.

Adoption: The Whole Epicenter, Nancy Parmenter.
Detroit Free Press.

Airport Reunion Ends 28 Year Separation Of Mother,
Daughter, James Dawson. Minneapolis Tribune,
May 8, 1983.

Babies Having Babies, Marie-Claude Wrenn. Report
on the Edna Gladney Home, Fort Worth, Texas.

Daughter's Search For "Lost Mother" (A), Carolyn
Delevitt. U.S. News and World Report, June 25,
1984.

Finding Birth Mother And Self, Anita Pyzik Lienert.
Detroit Free Press, May 10, 1992.

I'm 38 And Running Out Of Time, Paulette Mason.
New York Times OP-ED, Saturday, October 3, 1992.

Is Blood Thicker Than Adoption?, Richard Weizel.
U.S. Newsweek, March 20-22, 1992.

Most Adoptees Cling To Relationships, Felicia Lee. U.S.A. Today.

Mothers Often Seek Adopted Children, Judy Klemesrud. Taken from The Blade, Toledo, Ohio, November 24, 1983.

Record Of Adoption, Martin F. Kohn. Detroit Free Press, Sunday, February 7, 1993.

Search For Mary Beth (The), Carol Ann Berry. Good Housekeeping, August 1991.

Shadows Of An Unknown Past, Claire Berman. American Health, September-October, 1983.

Share My Joy, Whole At Last, Margie Reins Smith. Grosse Pointe News, October 4, 1990.

War for Baby Clausen (The), Lucinda Franks. New Yorker Magazine, Spring, 1993.

III. BOOKS

Adopt The Baby You Want, by Michael R. Sullivan with Susan Schultz.

Adoption, The Grafted Tree, by Laurie Wishard and William Wishard, 1979.

Adoption Too Soon, by Jeanne Warren Lindsay.

Adoption Triangle (The), by Arthur D. Sorosky, M.D.

Are Those Kids Yours?, by Cheri Register.

Family Secrets, by David Leitch.

How It Feels To Be Adopted, by Jill Krementz.

I Heard My Sister Speak My Name, by Thomas Savage.

Lost and Found, by Betty Jean Lifton.

Open Adoption Book, by Bruce M. Rappaport.

Search, A Handbook for Adoptees and Birthparents, by Jayne Askin with Bob Oskam, 1982.

Successful Adoption, by Jacqueline Hornor Plumez.

IV. ORGANIZATIONS AND SEARCH GROUPS

Adoptees and Birthparents in Search,
P.O.Box 5551,
West Columbia, South Carolina 29171,
(803) 796-4508. Contact: Karen Connor.

Adoptees and Birthparents in Search,
P.O.Box 6426B,
Greenville, South Carolina 29606,
(803) 877-1458. Contact: Mary (Crandall) Bishop.

Adoptee Liberty Movement Association (ALMA),
P.O. Box 727, Radio City Station,
New York, New York 10101-2727,
(212) 581-1568. Contact: Joe Soll.

Adoptees Search Rights Association,
Xenia, Ohio 45385,
(419) 855-8439. Contact: Nelda Gladden,
Director/President.

Adoptees Searching,
 P.O. Box 1774 Anderson,
South Carolina 29622,
(803) 225-0833.

Adoptees Together,
Route 1, Box 30-B-5,
Climax, North Carolina 27233.

American Adoption Congress,
1000 Connecticut Avenue N.W.,
Washington, D.C. 20036.

Children's Bureau of South Carolina,
800 Dutch S. Blvd., Building D,
Columbia, South Carolina 29211. Contact: Francis
F. Lewis, Executive Director.

Concerned United Birth Parents,
2000 Walker Street, Des Moines, Iowa 50317.

International Soundex Reunion Registry (ISRR),
P.O. Box 2312,
Carson City, Nevada 89701.

Operation Identity,
13101 Black Stone Road N.E.,
Albuquerque, New Mexico 87111,
(505) 293-3144.

Orphan Voyage,
2141 Rd. 2300,
Cedaridge, Colorado 81413,
(303) 856-3937. Contact: Jean Paton, Director and
Founder.

Bibliography

Askin, Jayne, and Oskam, Bob. (1982). <u>Search, A Hand-book For Adoptees and Birthparents</u>. NY: Harper & Row.

Brodzinsky, David M., Ph.d, Schechter, Marshall, M.D., and Henig, Robin Marantz. (1992). <u>Being Adopted</u>. New York: Doubleday.

Lifton, Betty Jean. (1988). <u>Lost and Found</u>. New York: Dial Press.

Savage, Thomas. (1977). <u>I Heard My Sister Speak My Name</u>. Boston: Little, Brown.

Index